MANIFESTATION
WOLVERINE

MANIFESTATION WOLVERINE

THE COLLECTED POETRY OF RAY YOUNG BEAR

OPEN ROAD

INTEGRATED MEDIA

NEW YORK

Cover design by Kat JK Lee

978-1-5040-1415-1

Published in 2015 by Open Road Integrated Media, Inc.
345 Hudson Street
New York, NY 10014
www.openroadmedia.com

To those who have helped me on this "word-collecting" journey—from the beginning to today, forty-five years later. Here, I speak of my wife, Stella Lasley Young Bear; my mother, Chloe Young Bear; my grandmother, Ada Kapayou Old Bear; and my father, Leonard Young Bear. This includes extended and close family members, like my uncles, *wa wi ta wi*, on both sides. Also acknowledged are my aunts on my father's side, including their mother, my grandmother, *Ko ta to*. And for their historic and cultural contributions to the Meskwaki people, special recognition goes to my grandfathers Jack Old Bear and John Young Bear.

CONTENTS

WINTER OF THE SALAMANDER

CONTENTS

CONTENTS

THE INVISIBLE MUSICIAN

CONTENTS

THE ROCK ISLAND HIKING CLUB

CONTENTS

MANIFESTATION WOLVERINE

---

*concrete poem

WINTER OF THE SALAMANDER

Akwi ma - na ta wi - a sa mi-
ke ko- i na tti mo ya ni ni - ayo
tte ski-ne ko kwe te bya i ki

There are no elucidations or foresights here
merely experiments with words

1

BECAUSE THE BLUE RAIN EXISTS

GRANDMOTHER

if i were to see
her shape from a mile away
i'd know so quickly
that it would be her.
the purple scarf
and the plastic
shopping bag.
if i felt
hands on my head
i'd know that those
were her hands
warm and damp
with the smell
of roots.
if i heard
a voice
coming from
a rock
i'd know
and her words
would flow inside me
like the light
of someone
stirring ashes
from a sleeping fire
at night.

PAINTED VISIONS

faraway trains ring the existence of time.
inside the cold end of a small rainbow
we stood like lonely eagles
huddled against each other,
wishing to ourselves a gentle warm stove,
images of our participation
within the human world.
all of us, standing in a cluttered room,
standing away from the sound of our talons
scraping the frost from the earth.

we turned to the people and mumbled
something about the little girl
who said she could hold her breath
forever and that she knew the very thoughts
of a blackbird with dreams of the day
it will skiprope on a sidewalk.

once those years of sharp rivers
took me to a place of caged bears
who sang an endless song to us about
the blank shield without our painted
visions.
wear what you are to us
through a safety pin over your heart.
the bitter knife will recede.

in the brilliance of summer:
the earth performs its life and death.
the house stands unpainted.
we stand on the bridge
made by the gods of the cold rock,
the cold underwater.

we regather a lost rainbow.
we walk somewhere near the lightning
and our hearts imagine themselves
as fire-burnt cottonwood trees.

to the north beyond the wall
of this room, a purple night-fire
burns in glory and our ignorance feeds it,
sustains it.

i grow back into a child.
i cannot name the people around me.
the differences in our life.
the things which keep us in circles.
broken pieces which once belonged
to us.

FOUR SONGS OF LIFE

1)   a young man

the blue rain
quiet in feelings
losing
nothing—showing no one
that i am cold
in this earth
singing
different songs
i never heard
from the same people
unable
to create or remember
their own
songs to keep

2)   an old man

i sang
to the warm sun
and cold moon
this morning
and offered
myself
to the land
and gods
for them
to
teach
me
the old
hard tests of living
all over again

3)   this one

i remember well
my people's
songs.
i will not
reveal to anyone
that i know
these songs.
it was intended
for me
to keep
them
in secrecy
for they are now
mine to die with
me.

4)   the fourth

a time
in sadness
within the night
holding me
and comforting me.
here i am
being
taught
to be
a man
with life
and old sacred
songs to guide me alone
and love me
forever.

CATCHING THE DISTANCE

she closes her eyes for time
and the land, slender with meanings.

with the razor flicking above her arm,
she said, the blood will come out
through these holes. it will be
dark blood. its color will lift
as i inhale through this horn.

i went outside with my tooth
clutched inside my hand.
i thought to myself:
she will be well.
last night these skies
were filled with light
and it felt as if i was
just learning how to walk.
the earth seemed off-balance.
i followed a silver streaking star
until it exploded.
i felt comfortable
seeing the glint from my teeth
come back to me
before it rested to the north.

and from the bottom
of a kettle my grandmother
tipped over, small fiery sparks
representing a battle between humans somewhere,
raced back and forth. even after she had gone
into the house with the cooked food,
i was still kneeling over the black kettle.
i imagined some sparks coming out
and dragging away the dead.

i was called to eat.
my mother sat on the bed
with her bare back towards me.

the powdery medicine rolled itself
into the blood over her wounds.

there are plants breathing wisdom,
offered by earth, blooming on this land.
no one will give the time to learn.
i see myself as a snowy haze,
drifting slightly, turning around
always wanting to remember more.
sometimes it is clear and the wind
brings to my hand, many choices.

as a child, colored ribbons held me still
and smoke brought the day through
the longhouse. thunder and lightning
made some of us cringe under the tables.
years later, i stood under its black sky,
asking the creators of this world to forgive
my carelessness. i kept on dreaming night
after night that all i heard was the rumble.

the kettle still sways on fire
bringing my fears to a small comfort
for i can wait until this part of me
is over. i know there is a reason
to why tomorrow will come.
when it comes, there will be no need
to speak of parts.

THE CLOUDS THREW THIS LIGHT

these horses were tainted and yellow
when dawn first brought the cold,
making my breathing like
an old man's, cautiously
coming through a blanket
soaked with tiny red suns.

last-night-rains came to
a black whisper, wove its tail,
and moved after my grandfathers,
still smoking the offer i gave
while they were here.

the clouds threw this light
into the horses and they were revived
by the rumbling in their bones.

i stand cradling my rifle and
notice the day humming, swinging
my little sisters to sleep,
back and forth inside the old house.

DOORS

all they say he saw was
his younger brother's silhouette
trying to enter their sanctuary.
if it had been otherwise
people would have been permitted
to live endlessly.
for four days the younger
asked to be received
cried
he was alive and not evil.
the door never opened
to which he died and was taken
elsewhere.
it is wrong to speak out loud
of the older who did not accept the offer
for he is the one i say my life to. . . .

RUSHING

yellow november
comes swaying.
i feel the hooded man
drawing move on my friend's
back. in his brother
i see his face. black
pellets drop to the floor.
we had seen its flood.
the time we lied about
the stone and how it
was supposed to have hummed
away from his head.
his lungs are now full with
the rush of his bundled-
up life. bits of bread,
pie and cake are placed
in a dish. i smoke a
cigarette for him
and bury his clothes
on a hillside where
once a fox ran beside us.
his furry hands over his eyes.
i can still see the shovel.
the thought of a shotgun.
i heard that in the night
a deer whistled out his name
from a cornfield and gave
him its antlers spreading
his thoughts through
the passive quails.
years later, as i warmed
the shadow inside my coat
over the stove, my mother
announced she had found
a spring and she brought
the first taste to everyone
who was there. in some mornings
as icy as it was, i washed my face
in it, sometimes thinking

of the hooded man and the fox,
the rushing sounds of a river
under our house.

THESE HORSES CAME

1.

from inside the bird a dream hums itself out and turns
into a layer of wind rushing over my face that needs
a small feather from the badger's nose to blow away
and create corners where i will stand and think
myself into hard ways.

2.

these horses came on light grey clouds
and carried off the barbed wire fence-post.
i am thinking about a divided bird
divided into four equal pieces.
the snow falls over the thoughts of each man.
in their stomachs the winter begins.

3.

the railroad tracks steal a distance
and the crows fly off chipping memory
from their wings. in my eye there are words
and i am reminded of a story i once fell
asleep to.

i aim my rifle at the sun and ask:
are you really afraid of children?

MIX THESE EYES

whenever it came that close
i never sheltered myself
from the sad
moving with the woman-horses
recalling those grassy hills
where sometimes
a day or night would lose
tiny wet children
and then taking
whatever appeared as a feeling
to a nearby stream and drinking
their reflections to forget
the spin inside old soft eyes
the constant sorrow of her mind
of grown sons and growing grandchildren
the wooden casings of three
curled tip philippine knives

when your eyes turn down
i go back
remembering how often
the number of days
my arms folded to the table
and my head how it disengaged
from me decided to close the doors
from long days

whenever it came that close
the bundled hair and the braided corn
came talking in unison
one time of the two brothers
who held the sun on its crossing
how one cried after
he witnessed a fish-spear slice
through an eyeball

i wish i was the air under the ice
children sleep on the floor

we can hear the whistling
of their wooden ribs

we knew the badgers and the foxes
were something more: they stood
on the other side carving the trees
into simple wooden bowls filled with hearts
divided as bear   thunder   eagle   fox   fish
and wolf
before we appeared fitting ourselves
into them

BETWEEN HIS FINGERS

selected women and their children
went over the hills to pick
berries to be consumed sacredly.

i sat inhaling the smoky protection
coming through the ground
rather than the coarse wood.

yellow horses waited discerningly
against the oncoming day
speaking of the stillness
which followed their decisions
and ours.

he took a knife, cast it to the air
and said: seek a tree
from it whittle a stick
find this *one* and make a hole
between all his fingers
drive the sharpened stick
its length and then bring it
back and tell me if the corn
he has planted will grow
to be used.

the river stood behind the sun
and passed to the sun a small speckle.
the sun took this gift
and soon understood its meaning.
in respect, the sun combed his hair
but in the morning
he opened his bag where
he kept things that were given to him.
things he did not trust.

it was windy that day and spider webs
were in the air offering rides to the river.

WAR WALKING NEAR

death designs swirl high above faces that are of disbelief.
a captured people dressed in red hold hands and hum
to themselves a strange song.
brown rain slips fast into a sad freedom
low in the thoughts of the old man
who visioned the coming revolution.

he tells to his reflection a small word
not to reveal that in the night
he controls the night enemy
night-enemy-who-takes-us-with-magic-medicine.
he heard the eagle with eyes of war walking near.
they say the spring air comes without much intention.

SEEING AT NIGHT

say these are the ones seeing only at night.

if the standing place emanates cold
enemy sent wings flap peculiarity
from tree to tree and behind will sway
the old woman covered into a shawl.

i woke early morning and it was dark then.
i went outside looked at the swirling
restless forest.
she arrived with her small kettle.

the little people on the hillside
again have not showed themselves to us.
i guess the prayers along with the tobacco
were heard and absorbed the time
they wandered near our homes.
no one seems to know if it's
the good or bad which travels
with them.

ahead, sudden sickness in our children
will make us inquire.

they are targets accepting food readily
from acquaintances really the ones
whom we should fear.
the medicine men of the north
have all the right answers.
they know how to stop spells.
i feel the beginning catching up
and so i must stop
and go.

ONE CHIP OF HUMAN BONE

one chip of human bone

it is almost fitting
to die on the railroad tracks.

i can easily understand
how they felt on their long
staggered walks back

grinning to the stars.

there is something about
trains, drinking, and being
an indian with nothing to lose.

MORNING-WATER TRAIN WOMAN

it didn't take much talk for her
to realize that her brother
was drunk
a couple of years ago
when the morning wind blew a train
into his sleep
spreading the muscles and fibers
of his body over the tracks
prematurely towards the sun
claiming another
after the long stillness of bells
now jingling with persistence in her ears.
maybe we convinced her
in accordance to time and place
about this life where we walk with but few friends,
feeling around for reception
at our presence
willing to exchange old familiar connections
with no forgiveness added to our partings.
perhaps she is still thinking of new methods
by which to end herself
this coming weekend or the next.
surely it won't be the same
as the last time she tried:
taking a bottle of aspirins
and downing them with a can of engine oil.
the people just laughed and said:
there are other ways, besides. . . .

one time before she went away
i dreamt of her
sitting on the tracks
attentive to the distant changing colors
of the signal post.
i knew what she thought and felt.
there were images of small black trains
circling around her teeth.
their wheels were throwing sparks
setting fire to her long stringy hair.

her eyes withdrew farther back inside
the skull of her head
afraid of the scars,
moving and shifting
across her ribs
like long silvery railroad tracks.

THE SUN AND THE MORNING

we stood that day peeling potatoes
for an old woman
and spoke too often of skimming visions—
as easily as opening your eyes
and asking for permission to walk
through the rain with your little bucket
to catch it in—
because you thought you had heard it
soaking into the window
and making strange tapping noises
as it came closer
after it had circled the house four times.
i mentioned my feelings
for trains
which reminded me of small whirlwinds
spinning across the backs
of old white crows
flying the night without instructions from their masters.
you said exactly.
i knew your fingers
rubbed the tracks eight times
spitting out your words
with bits of coughed-up blood to make things easier,
and hurrying the long way home
making sure that your trailing-shawl is not touched
by the sun's fingers
whose daylight can infect you with black rotting skin.
though both of us try to live everything
the hard way,
there was one
who tore out his heart so that the children
would live slenderly without troubles.
it will become harder
when you try looking for us
for we blend too quickly with each other.
maybe sometimes shoulder to shoulder
like two crows
who sit on the sand
with our bellies full with the found meat

sharpening our talons against the rocks
and then
flying back to the old and hungry ones
our beaks drying in the wind and sun
the crust unable to come off
when we wash our faces by the river.

OASIS

i often saw you with towels wrapped
around your head,
hanging over your eyes rubbed
with the shadow of woman's oasis smile.
at dusk, carlights always gave you
away at your usual place:
walking the ditches.
my mother said you cooked each meal
for your mother laid in bed unable
to stand, looking out the window
till night.
did you ever think about the white
arabian horses that i buried
by the stream?

BIRDS WITH TEARS IN THEIR BONES

the dwarf slept until the birds banged
against his eyelids,
but it was only after great effort
that they succeeded in opening
his hollow eyes.
their opposites flew out, black, ruffled,
and fierce,
needing the water from the cold
springs.
to them it meant life for their master
and a hope of reviving him well enough to walk.
he had been asleep all through winter,
trying to figure out the old ways
by which he once practiced his medicine.
he did exactly as he was told:
he camouflaged himself in the berry bushes
and he aligned his pierced fingers
to the three positions of the moon.
he achieved his partial invisibility
and he caught crows as they danced on skulls
with their bellies full with the horsemeat,
and he listened to them,
smelled the enemy-lightning in their breath
as they mumbled and cackled about the different ways
they held counsel in trees,
the effectiveness of the unborn horse
inside the womb,
how they killed themselves as they grew old
by asking gentle words to come down
as a hail of ice—
it was honor to bleed along the rainbows.
days climbed inside his head,
filling it with secret upon secret,
and smiling whenever his straw-like reed
penetrated the hearts of humans.

one night, as he flew about checking
upon the images of himself,
standing around the points of his home,

he caught a green light glowing in the pine-trees.
he released it after it had changed into a firefly
and he followed it hovering across the paths.
it circled houses he often watched.
after following it over several hills,
he began to realize that the firefly
was aware of his intentions.
the firefly stepped out from the shadows
and greeted and announced himself.
the dwarf felt cold beads of water forming
on his wings. when he blinked his eyes
he expected to see a person, but before him
stood a one-legged salamander
speaking in a slow and leisure way that it was he,
the spirit of the salamander who spread
news of death. the salamander pointed
to him and he saw his house on fire.

no magic he had compared to that of his.
he thought of his children and of the moments
he gambled with their lives.
the salamander told him to forget his magic.
the dwarf stood crying and pleading
as the salamander hobbled away.
he promised him but he knew it wouldn't work.
the seasons came and he absorbed the powers
of all those who knew no prayers to anyone.
he stayed away from puzzling funerals.
spells and dreams returned.
he remembered the last time he woke.
he saw himself on the beaks of small birds.
the birds cherished his bones and he would sing
of salamander faces, flat stones,
magical voices, and the frozen ice
over the river.

PARTS: MY GRANDFATHERS
WALKED SPEAKING 1970

white buffalo runs sleeping through snow and mixes
me into animal bones avoiding to be struck by daylight.

red colored evenings accepted the meat
thrown as offering over this man's old sky shoulders.
it seemed that while he skinned his kill
songs were composed from the difficult life
of earthmaker and he sat with a knife
eager for his wind
to carry body scent other directions.

there are in a house of many years
my shoulders held by fingers of the sun.
a mourning woman who sat in the continual middle
arrived in disguise as mother and wrapped a red
                                            blanket
over my ways and edges even after
i had explained to her that i had known
of her before and that i knew of her intentions
of splitting the day and night in half
                            before my eyes
of sending the man with horns
with the body of a horse
walking and dancing into our paralyzed dreams.

she combed my hair with the wings of the seeking owl
properly
in the forests away from the houses.
she sang of spring birds and how brown running
                                        waters
would signal to the appointees to begin
family deaths by witchcraft.
she showed me a handful of ribs.
i leaned too close to the sun and felt the warmth
of peyote brushing and pumping its images
into my blood and heart

                    of a birchtree
giving birth to crystal snowflakes.
i washed my face with the water from the thunder.
i listened to the reasoning of two crows
who had chased spirits away from men who had
fasted for fourteen days.
i thought of an intended life and autumn came shyly
bearing songs but no gentle children.

woman of the horses sat in my circles.
she created fire burning only on the occasion
when boars cleaned the skin of people
from their teeth beside green rivers.
the northern lights carried the meaning
of being far past the sufferings of night enemies.
old men inside rainbows offered no messages
but whispered of another existence closer
to a prayer than tears.

my grandfathers walked speaking in choices
across the black sky.
i stood inside them and released my hand
which held my words gathered into parts
of the earth.

SIGNS

the winter must be here.
everyone grows weary
as they change worlds
not knowing which to learn
or which to keep from.

my grandmother wears
her sweater even before
the day is halfway through.

she is thinking of snow
and the times she will brush
it off the green rock.
the hungry dogs and how unaware
they will be.

the fire will eat the food
in memory and for the strength
of her grandchildren.

i rub my face against the window
feeling the change will
never take the place for me
feeling everything i am
it will never be enough.

LIKE A COILED WIRE

i am sitting in a hallway
ahead of me i feel the sound
of my legs brushing against
each other through the stiff
new pants

like a coiled wire i am walking
through friends and relatives

we each had to tell each other
that we didn't belong
to be far away from home
away from the idea of what
we should be

in this hallway i woke up
into a fog wearing brightly
colored clothes and i found myself
again

even then i couldn't believe
the presence of mountains

and when after three days
had gone into my life
i decided to walk
to the mountains

i kept walking over and coming
upon hills and rows and rows
of houses

and the white rocks on their roofs
finally made me realize that the mountains
were too far

i thought to myself

they're going to take it
away from me as well

trying to fill the empty
spaces in my mind
i became the train i rode on
passengers without direction

racing through dark tunnels
gently in between and out of sleep
my body convinced we are home
because of the way the birds
sing and that echo

TWO TIMES

two times i've seen
the great water and where
the land comes to an end,
where the standing spot
bends to the sky,
where the bird's wings
shaped the last cliff.
two times i remember
seeing and touching stones
on the sand beside the rotting
flesh of seals.

two times i stood apart
from the shell gatherer
and unwrapped from the green cloth,
from its tiny leather knots,
my offering to the water door
of the man who rode
the spiderweb.

two times, my grandmother's
white hair. two times,
the grey waves of the ocean
brought the muskrat
and the newly found earth
together.

POEM FOR VIET NAM

i will always miss the feeling
of friday on my mind.
the umbrella somewhere
in the dumps of south
viet nam. in exchange
for candy it will hide
the helicopter.
franco must be here
in a guy's heart. i've
heard so much about him.
the closest i got was when
i machine-gunned
the people waist deep
inside the brown speckled
swamp. the castle where we drank
the sweet wine from giant fish bowls
has come against us. we knew that
when we killed them they tasted
the blood of whoever stood
beside them. some of us
thought of our families.
the cactus warms in our
bodies. the old mansion
where his friend played
cards has murdered his
brother and we see the stabbing
right through the door. while
i ran i made a song from
my wind. i have not held
this god beside me. only
this rock that i've often
heard about stays and at times
feel it must be true. his words
are like my dreams. they are eating
balls of rice in front of us.
i heard them talking a couple
of yards ahead of us. the jets flew
in v formation and they reminded me
of the wild ducks back home. once,

when i looked down, my wrists opened
and i wiped the blood on a tree.
i can only sit there and imagine.
they were ear close. the next day
i wore their severed fingers
on my belt. my little brother
and i hunted while someone close
was being buried on the same hill
where we will end. we hardly knew him,
coming into his family twelve years
too late. it was a time when
strawberries came bearing
no actual meanings. the bright
color of our young clothes walks
out from the fog. a house speaks
through the mouth and mind
of the silversmith. we saw the red
sand on his boots. what do we
remember of him? i remember he
said good-bye that one fall.
it was on a sunday. he was slender.
the burns from a rifle barrel spotted
half his face. april black is somewhere.
i scratched his back knowing
of sacrifices. the children
growing up drunk.

WOODEN MEN

the day is now here
she said
if you feel the cold wind
in your face
please know it's for you
to allow the need for
explanation
wooden men
of earth
that we are
cannot be mistaken
what it took to live out
our selection in
pointing at you

i dream of teeth moving along
the clear side of a fog
carving notches into sticks
my lungs regret the inhale
of smoke and ashes
smudged faces and misconceptions

for the spring
to will itself to produce
us good weather
it must be demanding
several tornadoes
touch the ground
and houses splinter
rapidly into
a thousand pieces
dead people tumble
in the air
amid the debris
of their personal
effects

i have tried hard

not to change
because i know
what it has meant
to me
how i
as a dark green river
has changed its course
i open my hands and
bits of sand slide
through my fingers

COMING BACK HOME

somewhere inside me
there is a memory
of my grandfathers stalking
and catching robins
in the night of early
spring for food.
the snow continues
to gather children
outside, and i think,
as long as they are moving.
the frost sets itself
on the window before
the old man's eye.
we sit together
and imagine designs
which will eventually
vanish when the room
and talk become warm.
he goes over the people
one by one and stops at one,
because he can't find any
answers as to why she took
the instrument and used it as if
she were one. they do not like
her much, he says, dancing barefoot
with tight clothes, taking the songs
into a small black machine.
it's how you breathe and space the song.
the same old crowd will be out
of jail soon, and then,
back again. the trees
will be running with sweetwater
and hard work is to be expected.
there is much error in the way
we carry our being and purpose.
we covered everything with his
conclusions and sometimes
he balanced his confusion
with a small gesture and said,
better to leave things like that
alone. nobody will understand.

i pressed my fingers
against the window, leaving
five clear answers of the day
before it left, barking
down the road.

SANTA ANA WINDS

i hear the ocean water
swishing inside my ears.
the winds continue to grow
hot. ash comes down off
the burning mountains.

sleeping all day,
nobody ever came to wake me
among milky answers.

i left a trail of spit
on a sidewalk untouched.
she has children
crowded in her kitchen.
by handfuls she stuffs
indian corn into their
grimy mouths.
like lovers we go to her,
determined.

everything would
without failure
end up in my room.
my brother would be there
sighing immaturely:
son of a bitch.

disheartened,
i agreed.
autumn.
ducks.
corn clicking
in their stomachs.

TO REMEMBER THE SMALLEST

listen to the words coming
from our elders when they mention
our blood drying inside us and how
it peels
shedding itself
the more we pretend
with each other
the way our legs tire easily
and how they collapse
as if by purpose when
in flight from legless
crawling spirits
who notice that we do not wear
turtle feet around our necks
their fangs are set to bite us
the intent being to release and extract
lies we have fed to our bodies
a minor part of life nobody needs
is the reply i hear
i try to make your eyes
blend farther inside mine
to make you see where
we stand distant from
our actual places
holding on to our phantom arms
the only comfort we feel
i ask for your name when
the feeling comes to tell you
of this but you are constantly absent
or else you reason that it's of
little value besides being late
i sometimes *speak* for you
and i think you do the same
because i have seen it in your face
when i talk about my veins and how
i have tied them to the dawn
and how i hang suspended
above the earth
refusing to eat away my veins
as you have done

MORNING TALKING MOTHER

tonight, i encircle myself to a star
and my love for the earth shimmers
like schools of small rainbow-colored fish,
lighting the drowned walnut trees inside
the brown flooded rivers
swelling birth along the woods.
i think of each passing day when time expands,
bringing the land against my chest
and the birds keep walking as they
sing wildly over our house:
be in this daylight with me.
push yourself from the walls.
let me see you walk beneath me.
let me see your head sway.
let me see you breathe.
everyone has been up into the daylight.

i walk over her head and remember
of being told that no knives
or sharp objects must pierce
inside her hair.
this is her hair.
another grandmother whose hair
i am combing.
there are paths winding over her face
and every step is the same:
the feeling of one who is well known,
one who knows the warmth rising
as morning talking mother.

in her hands she prepares snow for the visitor.
she sprinkles the snow into the bare hills
and valleys where in the spring
after the plants have grown
people with medicine eyes come
to lift the plants from her head
taking them home to the sick.

i remember as i was looking out
from my eyes that my eyes were like windows
smeared and bent out of proportion,
that the earth was curved from where
i was sitting. cars came and disappeared.
it was summer and i sat on a blanket.
i watched my grandmother as she came to me,
holding a skillet. she set it down beside me
and she fanned the smoke which came from medicine
crackling over the hot coals
towards me.

USAGE

she said
the plants
were in
shape of
birds,
moving around
at night,
could be heard
at times.
i never asked how
they were
used.

TRAINS MADE OF STONE

until that sun or that circling spark
which keeps asking for an answer agrees to
either keep still or leave me alone,
i will sleep without pain,
without condonation.
looking outside, there are prints
in the snow, but no one thinks
the snow can walk. we are him.
a final moment breathes and we are mixed
securely into the winter months.
the choice has been here,
waiting for my decisions,
whether i will allow myself
to turn old, spinning hazily
through stories just once more
to feel like a keeper of importance,
ignorant of the leaves changing color,
ignorant of where i stand.

there are two light-complexioned sisters
camouflaged with ash and grey cloth,
watching the roads on sundays,
hoping to catch a glimpse of my body
drag itself over the warm purple stones
on the railroad crossing.
i listen to the sleet.
i know which color best represents
the day, why the heron sights us
even before we round the river bend.

i can't be like the ones before me.
i can't make my mother see.
i know of her feelings
as well as the past.
i believe in this walk towards
the west after death, but that's only for some
who have suffered and prayed through their lives,
preparing.

three times i was the slender bird praying
beside a well near dawn. these clouds drifting off
were the doors of my friends.

the old woman was an owl
of death. she approached my mother
at the gathering and whispered that
one of her daughters would have trouble
living.
my little sister danced as a part of day,
leading the others slowly towards a time
when all things would be reversed.
i was away when news of her will to dance
carried inside, telling me that the river
will never swell and give birth to lies.
i have found life this way and i will leave
like one, knowing that it has not passed.

THE OTTER SWIMS ON TO OTHERS

it is still here, the four-day-old rain
cold with the vow of belief,
a need to see a certain glint from the sun,
a desire to smell the scent the seasons share,
an extension of the bright yellow buffalo,
floating and stopping over each wooded hill.

its light spreads to the sleeping children.
they nervously twitch to the sound of thunder.
the thunder who made these children.
and the hummingbird whizzing through the day
stops at the day's end beside a tall flower,
wondering what part he plays to the children,
to their guardians. if anyone will ever
use him as an instrument to both heal
and destroy.

nothing with human meat and sinewy legs runs
informing others of news.

out in the middle of a river,
there is an island and it was there
where i felt akin to the otter.
i stay away from him, but i eat the food
he brings me. i'm not anybody anybody's looking for.
i'm the person who came and appreciated
the worthless too late.

the otter swims on to others.

i look down and see the river rise
over my body. there are too many tests to pass.
i know well ahead that i'll fail this one and i know
of the man who will blame me for it. the others who
follow him, listen to him. without anything to
follow, my life is on this island.

once, overwhelmed by the feeling in the air,
i sensed inside the longhouse the turning of sky
and earth. clouds and hummingbirds to remind me
of my loss. i heard above the weeping
and the singing, the humming voice of a woman.

i breathed in her presence hoping to become
all in one instant all that is desired in a human.
from my lips i sent my loose words:

grant me any existence. pass me for others.
take the unborn child and let it be him
whose name will be remembered when the frozen
lake is chopped open. let someone protect
the coming seasons. remind whoever it is not
to be taken in so quickly.
not to be the fools we have been.

2

WHEN WE ASSUME LIFE WILL GO WELL FOR US

FOUR POEMS

my reflection
seems upside-down

even when the daylight pushes
my shadow into
the ground

it is like that

     *

this little house swallows
her prayer
through the green fire
and stone

i disappear
into the body of a mouse
sleeping over the warm
ashes

     *

i am walking and i
notice that the road
seems bare

some of the stones
are missing

ahead is a toad
throwing stones
from his fingers
whatever thought
he is following
we are
following

*

through the cracks
along the walls of this
house

the sun reaches its peak

our dishes begin
to breathe

THE CROW CHILDREN WALK
MY CIRCLES IN THE SNOW

the buffalo breathed quietly inside
past visions of winter
as he thought of one time
when he stood on some far hill
with a shiny red blanket on his back
warmed by a bird who blew rain
into his eyes and saw
old white wolves lying on their thin bellies
gathered into a circle and eating the ground
that bled as if it had been torn
from an enemy's shoulder during battle
or a child's heart
suddenly coughed up without reason
but the times then
were hard and too real to be accepted
like a grandmother asking you
to comb her hair in the daylight
and you know she wants to tell you
what she saw and felt:
there has been someone floating around here
last night
carrying a small bundled bag
pierced by long sharp bones.
it has waited long enough
grows afraid and wants to take another person.
again it has sent a green fire through
our small land
freezing ears and anything
within its glow stands still.
for only through this way
it can be sure of not stopping
on its travel somewhere
and seeing its shadow on the morning ground
with the sun ripping its face apart
and dividing the skin to the eager crows:
the crows crying like women
when they find themselves talking to each other

in their master's voice
their children throwing up small green pieces
of warm flesh
and looking confused when their throats
suddenly leap out at the thought of white wings.

THE WOMAN'S VISION

from a row of trees
i see her face.
she carefully examines
the bulges on her stomach.
she is a snake in search
of its den, of a man looking
for stories in the wood.
there is a glassy twin
of himself and around him
are clouds of his frozen
breath, drifting, and we
meet them on the road.
there is a baby in a cradle
designed with beads,
brown and yellow ribbons,
spotted symbols for stars.
she remembers the twin
and the man reappears,
carving the image of her baby
into a tree, heating his knife
over a fire, burning in the figures
of black, ruffled, birds,
turtles, to be sure the trees
fell down.

THE WAY THE BIRD SAT

even for the wind there was no room.
the wind kept the cool to itself
and it seemed that his skin
also grew more selfish to feelings
for he was like a window
jealous of the light going through
denied his shadow the sun's warmth
when being alone brought him
the cool.

the way the bird sat
dividing the weather through songs
cleaning the snow and rain
from the underside of its wings
was evidence.
in its singing the bird counted
and acknowledged the changes
in the coolness of the wind.
he somehow held the bird responsible
as it flew about taking in puffs
of air. often the image of blue
hearts in the form of deer
crossed his mind outdoing
all magic and distortion
of the hummingbird who had
previously been the source
of his dreams. the bird
who had tunneled through
the daylight creating lines
in the air for his people
to follow.

his thoughts took him out
into a cornfield where he found himself
bundled up into a blanket thinking about
deer. the hummingbird
who had been dodging the all-day
rain stopped and hovered beside

him before it intermittently began
drinking water from the leaves around.

having killed and eaten so many deer
it was wrong to blame his weakness
on the sun and wind.
to accuse anyone nearby he thought
was as foolish as the consideration
to once save his morning's spit
with the intention of showing it
to people as proof that his blood
and time were almost out.
he even wanted to ask
if it was possible to leave it behind
for worship but all this faded away
like the flutter of wings
he always heard shooting past
the shadow of his foot before it
touched the ground.

once his nose bled all day
and he saved the blood
in his kitchen cups
testing himself to see if
his notions were true.
he emptied them in the yard
and just before the sun left
the standing cup-shaped forms
glistened.
when he woke the next morning
he couldn't find one.
he looked everywhere.
on the grass
under the porch
until he thought the whole event
a prescience.

the daylight was full and the birds
walked through his yard
speaking to each other
and sometimes gathering

around the area where he had set
his blood.

it was strange as he watched.
each time they walked away
from the area it was smooth
and intentional.
in his mind it reminded him
of a ceremony and he left lines
on where each bird had stepped
where each had circled
what words it might have said
even the prayers it might have sung
and when the birds had sticks
in their mouths he saw the singers
with their notched sticks.
their beaks moved up and down
the sticks made a rasping noise
and when the women hummed
it was a song he knew very well.
he danced to the rhythm
as the weather forced him
to watch from the windows
of his house. most of the birds
had the faces of people he had met
and lost. there was one he couldn't
recognize. although it was getting
dark he could tell that one wore
the face of a deer. he was still
puzzled long after the downpour.

THE COOK

with the thinking of winter
no longer enclosing her
to her room, the combing
woman with the mirror smiled
as she idly watched the lard can
swing from the cook shed.
the kettle chains would soon
be unwrapped from the newspapers
and it refreshed her to know
she would soon be asked to
cook for praying families,
to laugh among the other
women.

the image in the mirror
worried her. it folded
her face carefully into
the sides of the apron.
here was the other person:
the one who knew exactly
what she felt and thought.
the person in the mirror told her
it was there for a purpose
and that was to double
her knowledge of roots,
hanging them on strings
from wall to wall in her
house, arranging them
by the power of their use.

when it was time to flow
the mirror knew first and it
showed her by fogging up
the windows of her house.
the birds with their breath
would then come, drawing
pictures, feeding her clothes
to the fire.

she felt the birds were
disappointed in being what
they were, always walking
up the trees, counting holes
endlessly, shining the sun
off their stomachs onto her
hands. she would caress her hands
over her face and every time
she did this, the rain would come
out from the fields, breaking
the winter and spring apart.
as the weather divided, the birds
would watch the combing woman's
lips and it reminded them of their
own shadows, three dwarfs
in search of tobacco,
wooden faces of death.

THE SEAL

in the corner of this
old woman's house,
sits another, of the same
age unable to speak
but able only to grunt
and moan like a seal,
doing a yes or a no
or a strange maybe.

people say when she
was inside her mother's
stomach, her mother
went to a circus, but
some also say it was while
swimming that she brushed
her body against a seal.
in time, the misfortune
is still here.

THE WINTER'S HEART

the winter's heart has been placed
into a small delicate bundle.
a young boy who first discovered it
underneath a blanket of snow explained
that it wandered aimlessly, that in
exchange for warmth and the attention
of a weedless squash garden, it would
promise to the clan a longer life than
others.

so it is here, beside the nocturnal fire,
moving about and taking in breaths of air,
instructing, but with it came a human,
half-buried, hidden in the forest.
on occasion the clan elders were
to have conferred with him,
but like thoughts from us
as we walk in step
passing each form and object,
he was quickly forgotten.

this is what happened.
they are no longer religious drunks
and the human in the forest has since
transformed into a mineral.

IN DREAM: THE PRIVACY OF SEQUENCE

always expecting the winter
to be a sad one
i slept after heavy eating of food
and waited until the portions
grew alive.
they sprouted antlers and formed
into circles,
fitted themselves perfectly
into my hollow teeth
and communicated to each other
about the comfort and quiet welcome
they were to receive:
of imitating the distance
between the sky, earth,
and the children
shaping a figure from the snow,
recognized and visible
in the eyes of old people
quickly running to their trunks
and fires,
unpacking the contracted faces
of relatives, arguing who
was born the closest to the dead:
long trails of smoke streamed out
from the houses that rested
deep inside the hills.
trees stood about with their arms
stretched out over their foreheads
blocking out the sun,
wondering why the children's
laughter covered everything
in the whole valley including
sound. the trees turned to
the old man who had been sitting
in front of the sun.
the old man right away thought
he knew the reason why the trees'
eyes closed when he met them
with his. repositioning himself,

67

he pretended to gaze out past
them. he knew they had lost
the question. relieved, he
whistled like a bird and then
realized much more the quietness
that was in the air. without birds
or leaves or anything to travel
in the wind with except his
acknowledgment which went from
tree to tree being refused
at each ear. feeling strange,
he stood up and saw for the first
time, children running in the open.
the multi-colored kites in their hands.
the old man was familiar
with the various faces in
the sky and once in his dream
the kites came as disguised gods,
needing the lives of children
to prolong theirs.
it is just like flying a flag,
running away from a fox, going
back through the hole you
crawled through.

outside, the depicted visitor
standing in place of the weather
gathers himself around me,
holding in each hand, two
branches, strings of dried hearts,
the coming hardship of death.
with a mouthful of ashes,
he digs into the earth
hoping to save his warmth
for the otter who sleeps without
dreams, or without me to stand
above him, reminding him
of the cold, the dark thin birds,
the memory of their consumption tied in
little bags.

forgetting the good
of the coming spring,
my fingernails grew long
like brittle shovels
and dug out the squirrel
and pheasant from my teeth,
thick and warm, resembling
rocks.
i thought of the forest
where the deer killed people.
i had seen this one man's body
lying beside a fence which
bordered this forest. it looked
as if they had poked after
the bullet with their fingers
tracing the clot. farther
down i saw the man's head
propped up against a tree.

i found myself between the airs
of changing weather
unable to distinguish what
to kill, layers of wind over my eyes,
growing old and uncertain,
skinning and cutting out
the kneeling children from
the bodies of animals.
i throw the food to my dog
who refuses to eat although
he knows it is a worship to his skill
and lets the others crowd in.
once, a boy with puffed-up
eyes took out the roof
of his mouth and sharpened
his knife on his heart.
smiling, he licked the knife's edge
and proceeded to carve for me
a boat with arms and legs.
all night, the boat
struggled to lift its burnt
belly to the stars. sensing
that the boy had fallen asleep,

daylight came, took the boy's
knife and sliced off the boy's
fingers, crushed them,
dried and sifted them with
its hands and breath until
they changed into trees.
the particles that blew away
from the daylight's breath
made the boy dream that
he had rubbed his hands
against the sky.

HER HUSBAND

despite irregular occurrences
and the sudden accumulation
of her years, she was content
to be inside her humid, small
framed house.
it alarmed her that she had
unknowingly removed her sweater.
a rare gesture.
stacked under the table
her canned goods looked as if
it would be a tiring job in
deciding which one would be
best to open and to eat.
the flies with their buzzing
wings made the place loud.
there was a peculiar sensation
in her throat indicating she had
succumbed to a fever
and whatever collected in
her lungs also attracted
the flies.
in the middle of summer,
she thought, today, a day
to have soup without crackers.

she had lived in the land all
her life and had seen her husband
some of her children die as she held
vigil beside their beds, unable
to revive them but pleased
their suffering was short.
she often wondered if anything
mattered to her, if she had
adhered to her spiritual
walk.

in her walks she found herself
in doubt and always headed toward

familiar roads to places where she
once grew.
these were barren places.
the trees which were there
in bloom and the skeletal huts
where she cooked in seclusion
were the things which remained.
the chickadee's stuttering call.

ANOTHER FACE

small eyes water on the branch
they have been there
for a long time now
thinking:
please move your wings
to show me i have found you
at last.

*   *   *

this rock halfway out of the snow
turns away from the daylight
and cradles small blue footprints
into its stomach.
at night, they mark the snow again
keeping close to the rock.

WAITING TO BE FED

she swam smiling in the river
thinking it was good that she
had come out here to be with the sun
going out into the air
and giving warmth to her sisters' faces
watching her from the sides
listening carefully for the hum
of human voices.
no one would show up here today
she thought. it was too hot
to swim with the sun
radiating on the wings of insects
flying in repetition
between shadow and sunlight
confused in their decisions
evident by the sound
of their open mouths everywhere.

through the years to now
she had known the river well.
sometimes she imagined herself
a rock under the water
surrounded by a landscape
that would bend the trees
through the sky
and then through the stars
reminding her of burnt holes
in cloth that protected
her hand from fire
while cooking for people
waiting to be fed.
she knew a place where
it was like this
where it suddenly became cool
and clear. this place
had often been mentioned
in her mother's constant warnings
about rivers.
like the insects and the sunlight

she released her thought
to a spiderweb drifting
across the river
breaking through the clouds
losing all revenge to the giants
lifting their heads in their watch
to her swimming over the cool
gushing spring
coming up from under the river
thinking of her stomach
and how it was growing fast.
the child swimming inside her:
the touching and speaking of two hearts
made her feel she could smell the sweetness
of the baby's skin in her breath.

in time she would be able to see
the face inside her stomach.
a dream indented on her body.
she took care of it
as if it were a god
as if the snow in winter
had already begun to take shape
in the hands of children
far from the staring foreheads
of their houses.
she knew it wasn't sacred
but everything in the land
seemed that way.
everyone took great interest
and care for her that she
could somehow make out visible
strips of gentleness gathering
around her body
streaming out from her family
a circle of suns.

she looked at her reflection
floating over the water.
it seemed as if the sound
of water was also the sound

of rustling leaves.
her sisters broke her thoughts
when they suddenly stopped
talking. she quickly asked
if there was anything wrong
but they remained motionless.
from a distance she could
not tell if they were playing.
it was a long time before
she found herself shouting
and hitting at the water
hoping they would start
moving. soon her sisters' hands
indicated a discussion.
she could not hear their words.
she felt her body drifting
away taken by the foam.
the water rippled to the banks.
seals crawled out from holes
she hadn't noticed before.
she could feel the cold
water as the seals swam by
brushing the bodies of her
sisters against her stomach.

she felt twisted in a dream.
there was talk around her
and she could sense by the words
being spoken that it was night
and that relatives were inside
the house being fed. each one
chewing and then
quietly nodding.
her mother's hand covered her head.
there was whisper from the root
telling her to be still.
she died as she gave birth.
the child lived without ever hearing
or speaking.
she lived in the shadows
of her keeper's house
and was taken care of all her life.

sometimes she would go out into
the daylight and rock her body
back and forth as she sat
on the porch.
a smile on her face.
her arms and legs folded to her body.
the sun deep inside her eyes
walking to the river.

SPEARFISHERMEN

the sun has melted the ice
over the river
down the middle
from the north
and south

it stops where
the men are filling
their bags
with frozen
fish

most of them
are grinning
every now and then
they burst out praises
to whoever
speared
the largest catfish

no one can believe
the spectacle
of all the fish
swimming
under the river
in cycles

unwanted fish
swim in packs
above dark shadows
of prehistoric
fish

men peer into
the water and complain
about the dull reflection
the silver coffee cans
are making

they curse seeing

the two bright spots
on the tail of the fish
disappear
in the corner
of their eyes

the sun has reduced
the ice into a single
narrow bridge
over the river

most of the men keep
to the side of the river
they're on
but there are a few
with courage who cross
from side to the side

trying to exhaust
all possibilities
of finding even bigger fish

the others patiently
watch their holes in the ice
occasionally they see
the spots
and every time
it's too late

the strain of the arm
muscles seems foolish
the prongs
from the spear
dig deep into
the sand

and every time it does
it is an ugly sound

STAR BLANKET

the cracks on the walls
of the summer house
divide the earth into pieces
of blue knots on a string.

we are in night
as it is outside.
sightless, i grow
into my patients,
arrange them in the order
of their warmth.

the sound of a bird.
its wings.
the flexing of my bones
makes the beans shake
by the woman's feet.
a single leg begins to move,
gets up and fits itself
over the cracks.

i see whistles
catching and eating
the gourds as they spin
and talk on the dirt
floor, nudging everyone away
from their boundaries.

with my fingers together,
a man loops leather
around them, tying them
to his. inside the star
blanket, i hear the wind slapping
the canvas over the roof.

the intensity of light
is felt and everyone grows
concerned, appoints

the door-faced man
to climb to the roof,
covering the night
more securely.

at my feet,
a row of sitting men
are level like trees.
i hear their wings,
sounding hollow,
filled with conversation,
boring a hole in the sky.
the smell of wood
everywhere.

swallowing a small copper
tube, i light up the people's
bodies and detect malignant clots
traveling freely like worms.

the tube brings back
the sickness while i grind
the red rock with my teeth
into sand, mixing it into
the grey and blue holes
of the woman's inner skin,
patching her bag of busting
water.

as the tube goes out
again, i feel the mouth
of a baby attaching itself
to the tube,
gesturing to me,
depressed with the one name
it has.

i fit my heart on one end
and breathe out of the copper
his name: two men lying
to the third.

THE PLACE OF L

i'm not without you.
it's such a warm day
to wake up to,
to still feel yourself
dreaming,
always ending up where
the dead wake unexpectedly
with the mourners
taking it naturally
until the one dead
loosens his blankets
and walks around,
sorts you out from the rest,
tells you it's no longer
important and sends you on
to another dream of less importance.
the relatives hold up their faces
to the day with smiles and false
attention to the children.
they'd like to have the day
go quick. there's hardly
any time to gather our thoughts.
my grandmother sensed that you
had walked by, stopping and entering
her house for a drink of water.
she heard you place the dipper
back into the pail.
announcing your absence,
my uncle breathes hard.
i picture the walls of the house
breathing. heat rises from the stones
on the road. all morning you had been there.
the sun warming your back.
your fingers touching the earth
for the last time. the girl who was
with you still looks at the hole
in her thigh. bits of grass and mud.
it still isn't over. i was up most
of the night, taking myself apart,

rearranging my head, thinking how beautiful
it would be to lie beside your cousin,
to have some people or passersby standing
around us. the gun between us. the sound
of a car coming down the road.
blood glistening between the cracks
of our grey mouths.

THE PLACE OF M

a short day has grown
into the sky,
balancing itself
between our places
of breathing.
the thought of warm
roomlight has left me.
the thought of our
hands against the house,
measuring each corner
and each window
has left me.
the snow melts on
the ground and the yellow
of corn appears in the eyes
of flying birds.
the food you left
for the wandering man
walks behind you.
the killer's car
sits under the sun.
its eyes skim over
the walls of the house
looking for signs that
will make it remember
but it doesn't find
anything except a boy
carrying a boy who keeps
on fainting, falling
into seizures.
from the fog, an old man
troubles his weak legs
to kick the stones alive.
his moist face attracts
you, tells you to leave
the past alone.
you offer the comfort
of your finger to fit
around his finger like

a ring so that he may glance
at it every now and then
now that he is walking away in his
father's hands in the form of five
sticks.

CELEBRATION

the little girl dressed
in purple,
a pattern of sealed eyes,
comes to the foot
of our bed,
signals her presence
and runs away from us,
dropping from her fingers,
a handkerchief filled
with well-chewed peyote,
fifteen cups of steaming tea,
wet circles in the wood
on the floor,
the name of the man who
chewed the peyote into
a ball.

outside, i see
through the frost
on the grass,
a snake,
coughing out hundreds
of babies in her dream
of falling,
dreaming of the young boy
who takes half of the green
roundness in his mouth,
hides the other half
on the bone of his wrist,
inhales the smoke from
burning sheaves of corn.

the snake is a woman,
her hair the sound
of horses,
an arm walking over
the soft white spots
of a frozen river.

she breaks through the ice
and two hearts float
to the surface.
each bearing her mouth
and my nose.
it was easy being made
to exist and to not breathe.

men with wings
of smoked birds,
porcupine heads,
dance under the plains sun,
under the lights
of mingling medicines.
the people in their dancing
pause to hear the laughing
of drunks, the other
drums along the ridges.

at home, away from
the celebration,
a girl inserts herself
with a clothes hanger,
smears her guilt on the windows
thinking of the deaths
of her half-brothers.

decorated children walk
away from campfires.
the cowboy-hatted singers
grow weary under the shade
of damp pine branches,
gather their heads
to the middle,
talk among themselves
about a trick song,
two deaths in one day,
and the girl whose
parents rushed home,
scraping the insides
of their daughter off

the walls, bending
the wire hanger back
into shape and taking
care of it as if it were
a child.

THIS HOUSE

i begin with the hills
lying outside the walls
of this house.
the snow and the houses
in the snow begin somewhere.
the dogs curled against each
other must feel they own
the houses, the people
in each house must feel
they own the dogs
but the snow is by itself
piling itself over everything.

i keep thinking of comfort
such as a badger stretched over
a house with its guts pulled
out. its legs over each corner.
it is truly a dream to tie down
a skinned badger like a tent over
a house, watching it shift
as the wind changes direction,
like the cylinders of pistols,
the holes of magnums turning
people inside out.

my young wife turns under
the yellow blanket in her sleep.
she wishes to be left alone,
closes herself within the dark
of her stomach, cups her hands
and sees what is ahead of us.
she senses i will die long before
the two of them, leaving her
without a house, without roomlight.

the yellow blanket, the house
and its people cover her.
the clothes she wears cover her.
the skin of her body covers her.

the bones cover her womb.
the badger feels it owns the womb,
protects the unborn child,
encircles itself to a star
and dies in our place.

IN MISSING

the stars in your perpetual face
reflect on the window
and they glow on through
to yesterday, floating past
the illusion of gathered boars.
the prints of my hand
on each boar collect
the snow as it delicately
drops from the sky.
i want to think the trees
are hearing me think.
i haven't seen my brother
for a long time. i keep
thinking that his time is spent
watching the air move between
the river and the ice.

there are small faces with
cupped ears looking for
tobacco. from the north
a man comes to us and wraps
himself in a blanket.
he tells us he represents
the starry night. he covers
his whole body except his legs.
his helper goes over the blanket
with a rope. we are asked to remove
our glass eyes.

even with the blanket
i remember his fingers were
entwined with blue material
and white ribbons.
he kept saying to us:
i am the wall of these coughing
sticks. i have flown down to
the woman who believes there
are children packed somewhere

in her belly. we've brushed
our wings up against her,
but she keeps insisting
that she must point at her
younger sister. there is a tree
with strings of beads all around
it. a girl cried and then we sat
still.

i imagined a white bird
imitating the old man's voice.
he could see its face. the suddenness
of her daughter's miscarriage. i feel
lost. somewhere i remember my grandmother
leading me up a hill. we came to a tree
and she pointed down at the ground.
we stood for awhile before we each
touched it.

FROM HIS DREAM

the air hadn't changed
since she last saw her mother.
the land was covered with frozen
rain. she knew a couple of days
ahead that the spring would disappear.
she kept reminding to her husband,
it'll have to come back.
i don't think it's really over with,
but he always seemed disinterested.
a look of worry in his eyes.
even as it was snowing,
thunder rolled across the roof
of their home and they couldn't
help glancing at each other
with puzzled faces. bodies
of disemboweled animals flashed
in their minds,
the children ran about in play
but when they ran into their father's
eyes, they could see the light
of their rooms, the changing contrast
of shadows, clothes that had to be buried,
faces of death, a knife burning in
the figure of seals on a tree.
the second time they ran,
the wind made sounds as if
there were people with their mouths
up against the house, talking.
as it grew colder, the snow made
more noise against the plastic
coverings over the windows.
when the children looked outside
they could see the clouds piling up
on top of each other, each group
darker than the other.
across the room where their mother
sat they could distinctly visualize
the changing color of her lips.
teeth biting into her skin.

they followed as she circled
the room, spitting the chewed willow
all around the windows.

their son had been gone most
of the day. it wasn't unusual for him
to hunt alone. he always seemed to know
what to do. old enough to be gifted
naturally to keep away from flowing women,
he had spoken about sliding down hills
on his knees, picking up the snow
to his ears and hearing the thoughts
of deer, bringing packed bodies
of muskrat and duck, the different
crusts of blood on his shoulder bag.

from a distance, his father
could see his tracks heading
into the thickets. small owls guided
their way through brush by the touch
in their wings. he remembered a dream
he had that morning of giant fish
and coral snakes submerged in the icy waters
of a river he had never seen.
he and his son cornering a small horse
covered with fish scales, bearing
the head of a frightened man.
its thin legs and cracked hooves.
somewhere in this land he knew
there was a place where these creatures
existed. he had also been told of a hole
where the spirits spent their days,
watching the people before they crawled
out, traveling through their arcs
in the sky towards evening like birds.
on the way back home, thinking his son
had circled the forest, he crawled
across a section of river which was still
covered with ice and fish entrails,
previous spots where he had taught
his son to use a blanket to block

out the daylight to lie there
with his barbed spear, waiting
for catfish to lumber out from the roots
of fallen trees under the ice.
although he felt a desire to crawl
straight across without looking
down into the river bottom through
the clear ice, something caught his eye,
and as he peered into the bubbling water,
he saw the severed head of his son,
the hoof from his dream,
bouncing along the sandy bottom.

THE LAST DREAM

the old man was already well ahead
of the spring, singing the songs
of his clan as well as others,
trying to memorize each segment
and each ritual, the differences
of the first-born, who would drink
the water from the drum, why it
was hard teaching the two-legged
figurine to connect itself
to the daylight, wondering
which syllable connected his body
to that of a hummingbird's
to have its eyes and speed,
why it was essential to be able
to see and avoid the aura
of hiding women. their huts
were visible along the hills,
draining the snow of its water,
making the winters visit much
shorter, but deep inside he knew
he had no regrets. the way
the bird sat, the way it cleaned
its wings, the way it breathed
told him he had kept his distance.
the winter had been friendly.
with only one dream to think
about, he collected the cold bodies
of muskrats given to him
by well-wishers and proceeded
to cut open their bellies,
carve their bodies into boats,
and positioned their bellies
to the sky, hoping for snow.
it was easy every time his
food ran out to hobble over
to the road knowing he'd get
a ride into town for groceries
and back, making little use
of his cane. it wasn't unusual

for him to look out his window
and see families bringing him
whiskey, bright-colored
blankets, assorted towels,
canned triangles of ham.
his trunks were full
of the people's gratitude.
through the summer and fall,
he named babies, led clan
feasts, and he never refused whenever
families asked him to speak
to the charred mouths of young
bodies that had died drunk.
he was always puzzled to see
their life seeping through
the bandages, the fresh oil
of their long hair,
the distorted and confused
shadows struggling to catch up
to their deaths. he spoke
to suicides just as he would
to anyone who had died peacefully.
he knew it was wrong to ask them
to go on, but he couldn't refuse
lives that were already lost.
everybody counted on him.
each knew that if they died
within his time, he would
be the one to hand them
their last dream,
the grandfather of all
dream.

WINTER OF THE SALAMANDER

i've waited through my wife's eyes
in time of death. although we have peeled
the masks of summer away from our faces
we have each seen the badger encircle itself
to a star, knowing that a covenant with his spirit
is always too much to ask for.

unlike us, her birth-companions have gone before us,
resembling small jittery waterbugs who keep
bumping into each other, unable to perceive
the differences between the eyes of their
children, the light-colored seals
camouflaged with native tongue
and beaded outfits.

we'd like to understand why we breathe
the same air, why the dead grow
in number, the role i play in speaking
to mouths that darken blue with swollen
gunpowder burns, chapped lips, and alcohol.
we keep wondering whether or not we'll ever
leave in the form of eight sticks.
we have waited until morning to turn off
the lights, hoping to catch a glimpse
of light chasing light.

there was a man whose name was k.
there was another whose name was m.
they knew they shared the same father.
the car of their killer sits within
the fresh snow. their grandfather sits
within the thought of a hummingbird,
women arriving at his request,
the mistake in the deaths of his grandsons,
the spell that came back.

they say: the mixbloods know of one
chance to be a people.

some of us, knowing of little dispute
in our past, forget and we assume life
will go well for us, life after death
being automatic. they are told
to absorb themselves into religion,
to learn and to outdo some drunken
fullblood's life. and me: like a dim star
i shine on and off in the midst of many
who have sat repeatedly within this line
of seated men, singing into the ears of leaves,
fresh twigs of the fresh green bean.

alfred and pete are still godless.
the morning has shown itself through
the windows of their houses, dissolving
the peyote in their stomachs, mixing
into the meal of sweetened meat and coffee,
half-man, half-horse, the green shirt
and the lamb.

turning eagle and i sit in the roomlight
of the salamander's two houses.
within the third house the windows frost.
at the beginning and end of each winter
we sit here before a body the size of our hand.
we made ourselves believe that no one
was responsible. we took the sound it made
from its last breath and we imagined a dwarf
hanging from the rafters with a lighted
cigarette in his mouth, reminding us
of the midpoint in the day.

the black kettle in the corner changes
into my young wife and she walks over
to the road with a small dish of food
and kneels down into the ditch,
whispering her mother's name: i invite you
to share with us this food.

3

IN THE BRILLIANCE OF
THE SUMMER DAYLIGHT

IN THE FIRST PLACE OF MY LIFE

in the first place of my life
something which comes before all others
there is the sacred and holylike
recurring memory of an old teethless
bushy white-haired man
gesturing with his wrinkled hands
and squinty eyes for me to walk to him
sitting on the edge of his wooden
summer bed

being supported and guided along
like a newborn spotted fawn
who rises to the cool and minty wind
i kept looking at his yellow
and cracked fingernails
they moved back and forth against the stove
and they shined against the kerosene-
                                darkened
kitchen and bedroom walls

i floated over the floor towards him
and he smiled as he lifted me up to the
                              cardboard
ceiling and on there were symbols i later read
as that of emily
her scratched-in name alongside the face
of a lonely softball player

remembrance two: it was shortly after he
                            held me
or else it was a day
or a couple of months
or a couple of years later when i saw him next
the bodies of three young men leaned against him
as he staggered out towards the night

i never knew what closed him
why i never saw him again

he was on the floor with a blanket
over his still and quiet body
above me there was a mouth moving
it was the face of a woman who had opened
the door for the three young men
she pointed to his body
this is your grandfather

and then i remember the daylight
with the bald-headed man in overalls
he too mentioned the absence
of my grandfather
i understood them both

i picture the appletree and its shade
as he was talking to me i saw a group
of people on the green grass
on the ground were table and linen cloths
with bowls and dishes of fruits and meats

the bald-headed man in overalls stood
in the brilliance of the summer daylight
his eyebrows made his face look concerned
or worried

later he stood on the same grass
he had been chosen to fill my grandfather's
empty place

the new colored blankets around his waist
and chest glistened with the fresh
fibrous wool
the beads reflected the good weather
the earth and its people stood and danced
with the beautifully clothed man
who was my grandfather
standing in between time
watching the daylight pass through
his eyes

from then on i only saw him occasionally
he would stand on his tractor
waving to each passing car on the road
as he drove home from
the soybean fields
or else he would converse with my two uncles
that the blood which ran through their
                                    father's veins
and theirs was unlike the rest of the tribe
in that it came from the beginnings
unlike ours

A WOMAN'S NAME

the faces who grew up
with me are still here.
i can only ask them
and they'll tell you
i haven't done wrong.
the huts of my seclusion
have all gone.
i've wrapped the cooking
chains in newspaper
ready to be given away.
through all of this,
the trees stand for a purpose.
they remind me of the time
i lived here, walking around
with my heart, my horse,
singing to anything
but afraid to meet anyone
who might catch me
with my mouth wide open,
the sun inside,
warming the bandaged
body of my child,
lost for good.

BEFORE LEAVING ME, THE POEM:
EAGLE BUTTE AND BLACK RIVER FALLS

for orlan eaglewalker, alfred rivers,
la james beareye, oreo, and weston wolfbones
whose songs come to us in the form
of small plastic boxes,
it can't be easy composing through alcohol
and vision, constantly thinking
of the newly released album,
each of them miles apart
from each other,
common lives and interests,
going over what they collectively
remember of that day they chose to sing
and record:
the food, the pepsi, or the coors
they might have had.
any organic substance that might
have coated their delicate and holy throats,
feeling the fibers restrain them,
depressed with hangovers and witchcraft,
learning the lesson of the man
with the voice of four men
all over again.

each of them would like to see
our faces, to see whether or not
we honor and respect their voices,
their years of dedication.
hot, dry summers. the many faces and styles
of various tribes, the famed fancy dancers
and their costumes of cowbells and porcupine.
the prestige which befalls any young girl
who by the end of summer discovers herself
pregnant, sitting through winter,
beading his outfits and listening to him
boast about his capabilities,
his bustles, feathers blessed with sacred
incense. the drums and their p.a. systems,

whirls of dust and medicine,
mingling floodlights of power,
scattered tents and new trucks,
drunken families.

aside from their songs, we learn
from the jacket covers of their albums
and by word, the names of their drums:
eagle crossing, redland, river boy,
sandyman, and thunderfires
of saskatchewan.

the day settles into the dark green
horizon of spring. the cool wind that comes
through our windows relaxes us.
we are lost within our minds,
within the new grass dance songs.
lying here, husband and wife,
in the thick smoke of cigarette.
each of us reaching over to the tape recorder,
turning up the volume of our supposed history,
a 90-minute memorex.

the loud and pulsating music draws
the white students to their windows
and they stand quiet behind the curtains,
listening to the intense sounds
coming from their neighbors' mobile home,
the indians. larry, the white man,
puts his arms around to the front part
of kathy's swollen fish belly,
spreading his fingers over the imagined aura
of creation and flesh,
forgetting his curiosity
of tribal past, mixtures of blood,
limitations.

far away from their shiftless breath,
farther away from the sweetness
of the baby's breath in kathy's breath,
there comes a song through the window

about a poor, drunken man in the rain
whispering the words of his gods,
riding across the earth with their horses,
demonstrating to the humans the importance
of seals, of men just as gifted as him,
singing at celebrations,
"it is only for you. we have no place
in this song. within this daylight,
dance for us this song we are singing
for you."

strengthened by the season's new songs,
my wife and i took my grandmother
to black river falls, wisconsin
unsure as to whether or not it'd
be a worthwhile trip, unsure of my driving.
sometimes seeing ourselves in a nightmare
of blood transfusions on the highway,
the metamorphosis of our bodies
into sticks. on the outskirts of la crosse
we drove into a valley of stone cliffs.
this would be the closest we would ever
come to mountains. i was overtaken
by the abrupt beauty of the land.
a selected place in time,
harboring the powers of the mystical
and the lonely, gods and dwarfs
peering down from the hills into our car,
fixing the memory of our faces
into their minds. the secret blessing
which guided our way to the northeast
memorial day weekend.
when we arrived the celebration
was just starting. people from all tribes
stood numbed by their tents and concession stands,
looking far into the celebration with greed
and jealousy, wearing their chokers
and turquoise, anything to help
some give the impression of being
indian. some of the people we thought
we knew walked by as if we had spoiled
their fantasies and right away we felt lost

and disoriented. we kept staring at each other
when most of the motels rejected us.
over hamburgers and coke, my grandmother
spoke, "some people try to hide their lives
as long as they can, but we see them
and help them when members of their family
pass away, it doesn't work to feel important."
somehow i knew it was the same for me.
i was no better, but for a moment
it came in the form of a small whirlwind,
rushing in my dream in search of pinetrees,
waiting for me to be uplifted and shaken
from the fog; to find myself within the cracks
of the whispering walls, undergoing test
upon test, wondering whether or not
we'd ever be together like this again.
the three of us, pressed on by the people
around us to go our own distorted ways.

THE SPIDER: A NAKED BODY
IN THE SUMMER

it would again come as if nothing
had happened.

i would enter it in my writings
as something whose force i had already
envisioned,
something we each lose and gain.

these walls are familiar
and then the next thing i'll say
is, i guess i have really
forgotten how it feels
to be on the other side
to have the burden
of a summer shadow.

i have seen a house of my own.
there is a station wagon
and we are inside

and i am waking up in you.
you hold my cubist drawing
above you.

did you do this?
it's pretty good.

if we have sex our hangovers
will go away.

only for awhile, kid.

i like the sensation that i am
having of remembering.
the light sprinkle of rain

stops above the pinetrees.
you kept talking about
your look-alike sister.
we can't do this.
i can still see the pain
in her eyes that night we saw each
other at the softball game.

i sat on the steps of the house
and everyone who drove by stopped
and expressed how much they felt
sorry for me, how stupid i was
to begin with, anyway.

you know, i have always imagined it.
somehow i knew last july
in the one moment when i was singing
in thought about how i would one day
drift back.

i wish i could get angry.
i did my best to invite the invisible.
in my mind i see chunks of apples
and burning cigarettes.
please stay away from the twin sisters
who cry in beat.

ALL DAY I HAVE SEEN YOU

it would have to be a very good reason.
i would see you off and then the next thing
i'd know you'd be gone, permanently.
everything that is us is represented
by the secondhand furniture.
i keep thinking i can withstand it.
it's easy to sit towards the east
on a summer evening, erasing the memory
of your absence with a cold beer.
all thoughts centered on the birds' airway.
the small dish of food which i placed
by the stream last summer was the closest
and only thing i did to remind the dead
and the sacred of my presence.

once, a one-eyed rabbit came right up
to me and i greeted it. another time,
a ground squirrel ate its way through
the plastic garbage bag. it dragged out
a photograph of us holding each other.
both of our eyes lost in miscarriage.

it would have to happen on a dull grey day
like this. i like to make myself believe
that i will have things planned long before
you have notions of leaving me.

you walk towards me from the west
with your head bowed down. the sound
of a bicycle leaves behind you. all day
i have seen you hanging clothes.
as you walk towards me you lose your
footing and i catch you by your wrist.
i ask how you see me. i always thought
you were kind. you know that one boy who
everybody thinks is a pervert? he's going
to wait for me until i finish school.

a tall and lone figure comes out
from the house and we hide behind
the station wagon, swatting mosquitoes
with the one towel which i eventually
give to you. i don't trust him. he is
good friends with the *fly* now
in sioux city.
how do you see me?

JULY TWENTY-SIX/1975

what could i have done if i had
been there? i grew tired of sitting.
the trees are there.
i can see the baseball diamond.
the power of one word of need
and coincidence.

it's hard to perceive sisters
beating one another senseless
with belt buckles, but i can see
the dents on the hood
of this car.

i need this trip.
i can't attach my thoughts
to anything specific.
we're going to be away from
everybody and we're free to do
as we choose.
again, the spacing in our lives
has shifted.

i open the glove compartment
and i discover a strange postcard
of an eagle landing on a cliff.
i tilt it and it repeats
the same sequence.
eight frames.

mounds of land race by.
i sense the long bronze body
of the car enjoying itself,
asleep and relaxed,
traveling over the stone
smooth highways
of eastern nebraska.

my cousin looks at herself
in the mirror and carefully licks
the taste of chicken
from her lips.

her son, the crow, talks
noisily to our grandmother
about the one day when they will go
back to montana to look for his
father, the reservation pig.

i think to myself,
what's the purpose of thinking?
i can't get rid of what has
happened. it's a shame that
i have dragged these people
into a troubled summer.

the brush in the land grows
more heavy and green.
we pass a carload of indians
headed towards the opposite
direction. macy.

we took the wrong route somewhere.
i don't know who's to blame.
i'm still pondering about
last night.

i see the approaching sign.
winnebago indian reservation.
my grandmother points to an old
deserted house in a ditch.
she tells of the time
when as a young girl she slept
there via an attempted rape
attack.

we are here on the second day
of this tribal celebration.

i fold my arms and head
against the steering wheel.
i've got to write a letter.
i drink a cup of warm milk.

dusty cars and staring faces
combined with the hot sun
hurt my eyes.

i start the letter:
this is from walthill.

THE CHARACTERS OF OUR ADDICTION

i am a long ways off from where
i'd like to be. days like today,
i dream which is the reason
why we are presently here.
my error.

there is a farm. i shoulder
a high-powered rifle.
through the binoculars
i see the two headlights.

three of my uncles are seated
around a polished table.
they are cheerful and they
enjoy the food.
we pretend things have returned
to being normal.

i selected this place.
i wanted to have a forest
nearby.
puzzles collapse in order.

all i want to do is to write.
something. the lawn mower speaks
for everyone. to the majority
of whites on this block,
it represents the spring.

one of the landlords just came
and asked why the electric company
couldn't get in to take a meter
reading. i replied, the door
is usually locked.
we'll make arrangements.

all right.

he takes one last piercing look
into the kitchen and living room.
as he walks towards the door
i pull an imaginary pistol up to his neck.

i picture myself in the desert
clutching my stomach with my fingers.
the stars are green plants.
my feet turn to incandescent hooves.
i take a bite out of the antler's
green bitter face.

we all share the last cigarette.
we untie the primal ropes from each other.
my wife places the bacon
between the paper towels.

a woman who has tried the duration
of her life to abstain
from the bad
falls into the corner of a house.
her eyes are crossed and foam
comes from her mouth.

her husband, the alcoholic,
picks the lint from his sweater.
my wife accepts a box of clothes.
it seems like there's always
a daughter returning
or else there's a baby
half-obsidian, half-clay
going from family to family
a short-loved novelty.

the furniture shines
with the day. i keep returning
to the land in my thoughts.
a shadow will refuse my offer
of wine and when it comes
into whichever house i am in,
we will not draw silence.

i sit here in abjection
all night. nothing planned.
towards morning i am still
singing long after
the station wagon
passed by, having seen
rochelle in oklahoma.
long after a different car
had passed, carrying the memories
of a film on bloodied oceans,
the time spent after being
forgotten.

we are a puzzle.
for one night, the parts
are mixed. the characters
of our addiction are elsewhere.
i feel a person sitting
on a porch. i am to someone
a voice, a sound.
we breathe each other's breath.

MEMORIES FOR NO ONE

i feel the oven warm itself
next to me. the electricity
hums all through the walls
of this apartment.
we are entangled in pipes,
miles of moving water.
my wife is in the living room
beading rosettes.
the television is in perpetual
conversation with itself.
i look at my silver
wrist watch. it's about time
to put the pizza in.
excuse me.

seems like nobody really
appreciates the coming spring.
it's going to be hard for everyone.
nobody knows what's going to happen.
people tire from each other's company.
seek new faces and times.
i like to think that i'm not like that.

ten more minutes.
outside, the campus bells
make music. students strain
their minds and bodies walking by
deep in eyebrow thought.
the fastidious moon hangs in the mist.
he will make memories for no one.

it is morning and i have just
closed the windows. the birds
crowd on the branch and they signal
each other. all of them sing directly
into the one window that's open,
simultaneously.
my wife is still beading.

the television voices remind me
of the way people speak when death
is present. it's soft and you can barely
hear anything but you know it's
important.

i see a figure of a man running
towards the door of our house.
i motion to him that i can't open the door
because of the layered ice. he approaches
and i see the deceased face of my son
fully grown.

on the wall there is a picture
of flowers and on the second night,
rain is falling.
nothing matters anymore.

i am like a naked spider
in the summer, feeding from
the rain, imitating the fresh sprouts
of plants.

THE MOON AND THE STARS,
THE STONE AND THE FIRE

i take my pants and shirt off.
my father and brother survey the area
towards the house before undressing.
it seems right for the summer wind
to feel good. i listen to my friends talk
under the clothesline.
heat from the fire warms
my legs. my mother speaks:
the stones are hot enough now.
she digs them out from the red ashes
and rolls them into the canvas hut.
she each gives us a towel and for no reason
i inspect it, following the hemmed edges
with my moist fingers. the moon
and the stars give us extra light.
i look at my mother as she hastily
rolls up the sides of the hut.
i have spent the middle of my summer
without my other *self.* i hope when i enter
she will feel how much i miss her.
is it right to feel this way?
i go through the opening in the hut.
i sit and cross my legs, making room
for my father and brother who i can see
settling into their places.
i hear a voice resounding from
the shadow of my father praying
for the essence of the stone to cleanse
us of the ill will around us, to cleanse
our bodies of any physical illness.
i see my brother russell hunched over.
he needs all the power which will come
into us. i don't want his food to come
spilling out every time he has eaten.

THEY ASK FOR RECOGNITION

within our lives
there is an impossibility
but as i am shifting from day
to night in your absence i am convinced
it is only one-sided.
it's regrettable:
the surroundings an eagle has,
eluding man, me,
a perennial tunnel in the sky.

i would prefer to turn back and look
where the stars and waves from the river
combine.
the triangle of our hearts.
the canvas which shuts us from
the universe.
we are complex.
there is an immense hate
that you have to be attentive
to what is being opened for you
whether it's candy or a can
of beer.

stay away from people
who can't stay in their places.
we see the time in their stomachs.
the clocks they have swallowed.
daughters and sons appear
and they ask for recognition
from sets of different mothers.
outside, we are not in compliance
to our divisions.

it's not the same.
did i actually know people?
this is only a river of clear blood.
no matter how many lies we record,
we still pack and congregate like flies.

we utilize simple and ambiguous words
to get by. we are accustomed
to the dream of our voice being wound
around a small, notched stick
buried under the fall's foliage.
it has a song of jealousy,
disparity,
the sound of two illiterate sisters
in flight.

in the weeks ahead i grew thin.
today i bow my head,
explain to myself:
spirits of houses and unseen children
equal a father and his sons.
i observe my voice being dug up
from the past.
on a certain spot along the ridge
on this hill there is a hole
in the ground where it once held
smoldering ashes, a smooth, ageless
rock.

IN DISGUST AND IN RESPONSE TO INDIAN-TYPE POETRY WRITTEN BY WHITES PUBLISHED IN A MAG WHICH KEEPS REJECTING ME

you know we'd like to be there
standing beside our grandfathers
being ourselves
without the frailty
and insignificance of the worlds
we suffer and balance
on top of now
unable to detect which to learn
or which to keep from
wearing the faces
of our seasonal excuses
constantly lying to each other
and ourselves about just how much
of the daylight
we understand
we would be there:
with the position of our minds
bent towards the autumn fox
feasts
feeling the strength and prayer
of the endured sacred human tests
we would set aside the year's
smallpox dead
whole and complete
with resignation
like the signs from the four legs
of our direction
standing still
sixty years back in time
breathing into the frosted lungs
of our horses the winter blessings
of our clan gods

through dependence
they would carry our belongings
and families to the woodlands
of eastern iowa to hunt our food
separate and apart
from the tribe
following and sometimes using
the river to cleanse the blood
from our daughters and wives
not knowing that far into
our lives we'd be the skulls
of their miscarriages
as a result:
the salamander would paralyze
our voice and hearing
under instruction
our sons the mutes would darken
their bodies with ash and we'd assist
them erect sweatlodges with canvas
water plants fire and poles
from the river
the scent of deer and geese
the hiss of medicine
against the heated rocks
belief would breathe into their bodies
camouflage and invisibility

somewhere an image of a woman's hand
would lunge out from the window
of a longhouse
and it would grab from our fingers
the secret writings of a book
describing to the appointee
the method of entering
the spirit and body
of a turkey
to walk at night in suspension
above the boundaries of cedar incense
to begin this line of witchcraft
traveling in various
animal forms
unaware of the discrepancy

127

that this too is an act of balance
a recurring dream of you
being whole and complete
sending the glint of your horns
into the great distances
of the gods
acquainting yourself with ritual
and abandonment of self-justification
to realize there is a point
when you stop being a people
sitting somewhere and reading
the poetry of others come out easily
at random
unlike yours which is hard to write
to feel yourself stretch
beyond limitation
to come here and write this poem
about something no one
knows about
no authority to anything

WE ARE DARKNESS ITSELF

we are darkness
itself

we are sitting
propped against
a wall

we are holding
our knees up against
our bodies

beside us
lies an overturned
figurine

someone advises us
if we hold it
and sing with it

we are preparing
for when we die
its use will be seen

as a spark

going in circles
and there shouldn't
be any misidentification

you are the only one
here

it doesn't matter
if your father
uncle

or brother attends
and shakes the instrument

and sings

the old man with
the beard and metal
glasses
dances with his bowlegs
and hunched back over
the earthen floor

he tells me
for us
it can be too late

through his alcoholic
breath i believe him

the whites can always
catch up with their
belief

if you feel you have
to begin
do so now

or else you will
be forever
in repentance

and when the time comes
after your death
what will you
do when you
are
asked by the *one*
who checks into the past
about your life

and if you followed
what you are supposed
to

i will do as i have
done all my life

i will stand
with my head down

i will shrug my shoulders
declare my love for all
those who went and passed
this way

before me

4

THE SOUND HE MAKES–THE SOUND I HEAR

IT SEEMS AS IF WE ARE SO FAR APART

it has been a steady thing now.
the cars drive by and the houses
and to whom they will be given
becomes a pathetic problem.
i keep looking in magazines.
last night i found an ad for
a chain saw and included
was a mechanical attachment
which enabled one to trim
logs into rectangles.
this would be a house
for us. a log cabin
in the pinetrees.
one room would be enough.
what would it represent?
four symmetrical walls of wood.
small windows.
the daylight coming in
with the morning.

there are two people
who live within those pinetrees.
we are all contrivances.
times when we can never
pinpoint what we are.
most depend on pretenses.

i can't live in ideal situations.
i have fallen off somewhere.
i am doing something which
cannot fit into what i foresee.
i am in balance on top of a frame.
it is a wall on the east side
of a house. i can see the adjacent rooms.
the fresh smell of pine.
sawdust. the strain and the effort
of two shadows.

it seems as if we are so far apart,
living here, in this house we share.
the children who survived the undertakings
of our night-enemy inhabit distant towns.
it still isn't too far.
i am incessantly afraid for them.
i am witness to a nocturnal fire.
small sticks are implanted
in the ground. there is a man stooped
over them, conversing.
on the spot where he is,
i have sensed before there
was some sort of dwelling.
this man has chosen a face
he'll carve from a tree.
as usual the hours pass each day
and i discover myself contemplating
my fate. i somehow seem satisfied
when cars pass on the road
frantically, stopping at each
neighborhood, informing the people
of the drunks who shot and killed
one another. i stand unencumbered
smoking a cigarette.

there will never be an answer
to the individual who wakes up dead.
families rush to other tribal healers.
spells and incantations are congested
with smoke and fire, speedometers,
gas stations, farmland.
the brown stringy root
goes out from the mound
in the earth and tunnels itself
into the tender feet of a girl.
her feet swell. another tunnels
itself into a finger which pulls
a trigger of a gun, independently,
exploding and sending the blood
of someone's son to the stars.
in a distant town, an old emaciated man
reinforces his prayer before the nurses

enter his cubicle, checking the plastic
that holds and nourishes his body.
deaf, he continues his homage
to the guardian bird.
to the nurses, it is simply
entertainment. somewhere else,
a boy gets off an elevator.
two unknown assailants brandishing
knives shove him against the wall.
the skin from his face gently peels
and falls onto the carpeted floor.
the nurse smiles at the old man.

lightning walks along its own path.
the cottonwoods are charred
and as i pass by them before
the sun ascends,
they conjointly point to me
and i can hear their accusations,
blaming me for the death
of a human and a tree.
never place the two together.
i am on this earth for no reason
other than to succeed and to practice
it. people come to me and as their
elder i can ascertain in their discussion
the strong grudge and dislike for all
who surpass them in their ambitions.
i see the young girl who has married
into the family. i sense the minute
sewn-on bundle in the corner
of her printed apron. she,
like the others, has been sent.
there is a man who can change into
a toad. from the north, i see the lights
in the eyes of dwarfs. after
the alcoholics have passed out
in their cars, the dwarfs come out
from the ditches. they brush their
moist hands against the alcoholics'
shiny faces.

I TOUCH A GENTLE DEER

i touch a gentle deer
on the neck with my cold hand.
it informs me of the lines
in the river.
the frozen bait
at the close of october.
from my mother
i hear:

you will never possess
anything if you make
alcohol your being.

you will subsequently
lose whatever else
is left of you.
the tribe has no one
particular characteristic.
none were created from
our creator.

only after and as separates.

like yours
the new cars on the road
are only a hazard for those
who walk or drive

unaware of your
distorted presence.

money is good and it came
in due time, however its origin
and intent. i hope no one finds
pain within this.

the water numbs

my fingers and i have
trouble loading the cylinder
of my pistol.

the cool breeze comes down
along the side of the pinetrees.

i am in favor of the fluctuating
moon.

usually it fades away.
i think of the divisions
within the lives
of people.

i picture triangles
descending from the moon
and they surround people
who consider themselves
different

from the rest.
sometimes there are just
families. sometimes it involves
dependence. a commitment.

once i walk through
these demarcations
it will confuse the moon.
mouths on the somber faces
of people will become rampant.

the owl doesn't call out
again. even though i try
not to think of it,

i see the owl and myself.
the sound he makes.
the sound i hear.

A POOL OF WATER,
A REFLECTION OF A SUMMER

from the very beginning of the summer,
we sat beside the brown river while it flooded.
we imagined great suspended fish under the rapids
and foam, taking the bait into their mouths
and sending the vibrations of their power
through our lines into our hands.

and the man who gave away dreams died along
with his songs, his memory, the clans.
there was a man who sat beside him,
a student who boasted about his mental
capabilities of remembering the songs
and their sequence. how he could outsing
the old man.

being afraid to see his still presence,
we fished that day. this wasn't the first for me.
it was a time to replace reality with the ardor
of a hunt. the sand from the beach drifted pebble
by pebble into the rushing river.

once when i went to a funeral for two people,
i bid them farewell in english. i wanted to stop
and start over. i felt disconcerted as i walked away
from them, but the line kept moving.
many wanted to put the day behind them.

in the hot misty haze with our barefeet and backs,
we heard what sounded like talk and then singing.
i abandoned the idea of nightfishing,
completely forgot about the fish
who had broken our 30-pound test
three times.

later on, the student of dreams will sit in silence.
no songs will slip into his mind. it will be awkward.

he will only sit there and remember the man who gave
away dreams.

on a bend where once a boat spun itself around
with three men aboard, we sat and i greeted
a snake swimming across, but it quickly changed
direction and came right in front of us.
in an act of appeasement and fear, i threw
my bait, a dead mangled frog, towards its mouth.
it dived and we never saw it again.

i feel it is poetry swimming under the shallow
river. a time imprinted into one's mind:
a last beam of sunset between a valley
of trees filled with hovering birds.
insects darting across the river.
a snake projecting its body from the water
towards your face.

we talked to the ancient paratrooper.
he pointed to the ledge five feet above us:
i used to come here with my brothers,
pulled up a lot of flathead. of course,
it was considerably deeper then.

i remembered hearing my friend speak
of the dynamite blast carrying the water
from the dam up into the sky over the hills.
i wished for some magic to come into us
and to lead us to the fish who chose
to remain behind. fish we would never see.

IN VIEWPOINT: POEM FOR 14 CATFISH AND THE TOWN OF TAMA, IOWA

into whose world do we go on living?
the northern pike and the walleye fish
thaw in the heat of the stove.
it wasn't too long ago
when they swam under the water,
sending bursts of water and clouds
of mossy particles from their gills,
camouflaging each other's route—
unable to find the heart to share
the last pockets of sunlight
and oxygen,
stifled by the inevitable
realization that the end is near
when man-sized fish slowly tumble up
from their secretive pits.
i, and many others, have an unparalleled
respect for the iowa river even though
the ice may be four to five feet thick,
but the farmers and the local whites
from the nearby town of tama and surrounding
towns, with their usual characteristic
ignorance and disregard, have driven noisily
over the ice and across our lands
on their pickups and snowmobiles,
disturbing the dwindling fish
and wildlife—
and due to their
own personal greed and self-
displeasure in avoiding the holes
made by tribal spearfishermen in
search of food (which would die
anyway because of the abnormal weather),
the snowmobilers ran and complained like
a bunch of spoiled and obnoxious children
to the conservation officer, who, with
nothing better to do along with a deputy
sheriff and a highway patrolman, rode out

to tribal land and arrested the fishermen
and their catfish.

with a bit of common sense,
and with a thousand other places
in the vast state of iowa to play toys
with their snowmobiles in, and with the winter
snow in well overabundance, they could have gone
elsewhere, but with the same 17th century
instincts they share with their own town's
drunken scums who fantasize like ritual
each weekend of finally secluding and beating
a lone indian's face into a bloody pulp,
they're no different except for the side
of railroad tracks they were born on
and whatever small town social
prominence they were born into.
it is the same attitude shared by lesser
intelligent animals who can't adapt
and get along with their environmental
surroundings.

undaunted, they gladly take our money
into their stores and banks, arrest
at whim our people—
deliberately overcharge us,
have meetings and debates as
to how much they should be paid to educate
our young.
why the paved streets as indicated
in their application for government funds
will benefit the indians.
among them, a dentist jokes and makes claims
about indian teeth he extracted solely
for economics.
the whites will pick and instigate
fights, but whenever an indian is provoked
into a defensive or verbal stand
against their illiterates,
or because he feels that he has been
unjustly wronged for something he has been

doing long before their spermatozoa set
across the atlantic (polluting and bloating
the earth with herbicides and insecticides),
troops of town police, highway patrolmen,
and assorted vigilantes storm through
indian-populated taverns, swinging
their flashlights and nervously holding on
to the bulbous heads of their nightclubs
with their sweaty hands, hoping
and anxiously waiting for someone
to trigger their archaic desires.
state conservation officers enter
our houses without permission,
opening and taking the meat and the skins
of our food from our cooking shacks
and refrigerators.
sometimes a mayor or two will deem it necessary
to come out and chase us and handcuff us over
our graveyards. the town newspaper overpublishes
any wrong or misdeed done by the indian
and the things which are significantly
important to the tribe as well as to the town,
for the most, ends up in the last pages,
after filling its initial pages
with whatever appeals to them as
being newsworthy and relevant indian
reading material.

unfortunately, through all of this,
some of *our* own people we hire, elect,
or appoint become so infected and obsessed
with misconceptions and greed, that they
forget they are there for the purpose
of helping us, not to give themselves
and each other's families priorities
in housing, education, and jobs.

altogether, it's pathetic seeing the town
and seeing mature uniformed and suited men
being led astray by its own scum, hiring
and giving morale to its own offspring scum

to make it right for all other scums
to follow.

they can't seem to leave us alone.
until they learn that the world and time
has moved on regardless of whether they still
believe and harbor antiquated ideas and notions
of being superior because of their pale light skin
alone, and until they learn that in their paranoia
to compare us to their desensitized lives,
they will never progress into what they
themselves call a community,
or even for the least,
a human.

IT IS THE FISH-FACED BOY WHO STRUGGLES

it is the fish-faced boy who struggles
with himself beside the variant rivers
that his parents pass on their horse
and wagon. he sees the brilliant river.
at times it turns invisible and he sees
fish he has never seen before.
once, somewhere here he had dreamt
of a wild pig killing his mother and
sister. it chased him into the river
and he swam to the other side and stood
on the beach, wiping the water from his face.
two others came and encircled him.
the dream ended under the river
where he walked into a room
full of people dressed in sacks.
the morning wind chilled his languid body.
he peered out again. birds hopped along
the frosted grass. he remembered what
the submerged people said to him when
he walked into the room: we've been
expecting you.
large glistening fins filled
his eyes with the harsh sunlight.
he felt his lungs expanding.
the ribs from his body tilted
at an angle away from the ground.
the fish in the river, a spectacle.
he sat back against the rocking
sideboards of the wagon.
he noticed his father's black hat
and his mother's striped wool blanket
bouncing in the ride.
as they crossed the iron bridge
he felt the tension from his body
subside. fog from the openings
in the river drifted into the swamps.
the road led them through a forest.

he thought of invisibility.
the web between the bone spines of the fish
were intercrossed with incandescent fiber.
their jaws sent bursts of water
down to the river bottom.
clouds of mud and sediment
settled beside white needlepoint teeth.
he could faintly hear the barking of dogs.
he knew they were nearing home
from the permeating scent
of the pinetrees. it occurred to him
that the trees and the scent were an
intrinsic part of the seasons.
these were moments when he questioned
his existence. for awhile he pictured
awkwardly dressed people. they were standing
motionless beside long tables.
the impression was, they were ready
to eat but there was no food.
he had seen the long tables somewhere.
the wagon stopped. his father stepped
down from the wagon and carried him
into the summer house. it was warm inside.
huge poles which supported the roof
stood in dark brown color absorbing
the constant smoke from the fire.
far ahead in time, his grandson
would come down from the lavender hills
with the intention of digging out the poles
to carry on the memory under a new roof.

he knew it was the next day
when he woke. he could hear the chickens
shuffling about. it was no longer warm.
the daylight dissipated as it came in
through the hole in the center
of the roof.
he turned on his side
and bumped into a small tin bucket.
he reached over and drew it close.
at first smell,
he couldn't define it, but gradually

as he slushed it around, he recognized
his vomit. yesterday's food.
suspended above the door
was a dried head of a fish.
its face a shield, the rainbow-
colored eyes. the teeth were constructed
with blue stone. he knew its symbols
represented a guardian.
white painted thorns and barbs stuck
out from its gills. lines of daylight
rushed through the cracks in the walls.
the smoke-darkened poles were ornately
decorated. the door moved against the force
of the centered breeze. the cool odor
of the pinetrees chilled his entire body.
he pulled his thin blanket closer to him
and he attempted to walk to the door.
for each step he took, he forgot
through the next one. he could faintly
distinguish what sounded like the cracking
of ice over the flapping of wings.

his father stood above the ice
with a spear in his arms. his eyes affixed
to the opening. the giant fish swam by
piled on top of one another. some were
luminous. others swam so close together
they resembled clouds. there were even
a few who quickly swallowed what looked
like intestines. the ones who had their
mouths closed led long streamers
of this substance and it camouflaged
whoever followed behind. these were the fish
who represented a power and a belief.
the season was coming sooner than
anyone had anticipated.
the people in the hills
completely forgot their ceremonies
yet you saw them everywhere, here, to observe.
the women were along the banks
of the river tying long straps
of leather around the deer hooves

on their feet.
the men in their dried speckled
fish heads hummed as they scraped blue
curls of ice with their stone teeth.
small children covered each mark
on the ice. fresh water was refilled.
underneath, the fish swung their tails
side to side, alert.
the women in their deer hooves
walked onto the ice.
the men in their fish heads
began to sing and the small children
after drinking what remained of the water
ran ahead pointing out the giant fish.

IN EACH OF US

in each of us
when we look out into the world
it is the same thing
no one tries to be lonely
the limitations are there
for us to confront
throughout our lives
no one questions
the burden
of finding
a solution to why
the occult and the belief
of a changing tribe
mix

i once wrote
of myself in a paper
a circle within a circle
an encounter with the isolation
caused by living beside
the railroad tracks

in a small light-brown house
i sketched out my abstractions
my brother came with the intent
of living with me through
the winter while he worked
loading plastic pipes
into trucks
he stayed for
a couple of nights
one morning i woke up
and i finally found out nothing
could ever be accomplished
there

i walked around on the tile floor
the dull electric light hummed erratically

above me
outside it was raining
i pictured a dying animal
in my mind
it fed on the sickness
it was dying from

i was never old then
it was just nervousness
a feeling as if i would never
have another opportunity
to grasp what represented
an escape from the gradual
settling of my life

i felt my body dissolving
whatever was left of me
floated over a river

the streets were black
from the rain
i blessed the pistol
in the dresser

NO ONE CAN DENY
THE STRONG FORCE

no one can deny the strong force
of the river under the ice.
where there are openings,
sheets of ice lift their jagged
bodies up into the wintry air
to take an occasional
but detailed glimpse of us.
we can hear someone amused.
up ahead, we see a glow.
we trudge deeper into the shade
of the willows, of the badger.

the cold stinging wind freezes our eyelids.
we wrap our lips around the willows.
we fall asleep to the sounds
of our backpacks whipping
in repetition across the snowdrift.

each winged object alarms us.
once, there was a venerable name
for each serpent.
everyone with their reasoning intact
carried their belongings on their backs.
water and something to eat.

so much for the thought of surviving
its winter.

we had been raised believing in the omen
of the multi-colored tempestuous badger.
we see the painted scales of the fish
he rides.

the roof above us is similar to his.
spots of light come through
and we stand within the continuous

design of the clouds, wind,
and the sun.

the music we sing represents our struggle.
at first, it is a series and then it
culminates to one total.
from great distances, people arrive
and we are told to respect them
for they have retained the capacity
to cure anything.

we embarrass ourselves by joining
in song with them.
passive moments with them were contradictions.

it makes the people who stayed away
happy. of course, it doesn't mean much.
we are all bonded within the same aspect
of waiting.

even before anything ever became
important, we were living as if we knew
what the reasons were.
children grew around us
and we were told it was important
despite the fact they were fatherless.
some fathers we knew,
others we never met.

each child was different from
its brothers and sisters.

she remembers the room where she followed
the hand of her father
traveling up the walls.
he would be there standing headless
near the ceiling, whistling songs.
the hand i followed was old and wrinkled.
it pointed to a bundled object
in the corner.

i remember the dried head
of the fish and there were pictures
on the wall around it,
signifying the mystical world
it came from.

she later realized that she had been
deliberately lied to and that the hand
she followed was a spider.
the same happened to me.
both had nothing to do with what
we were looking for.

we've been told he is persistently evasive
that the river would be the most obvious
place he would be.

we sat up most of the night.
sharpening the barbs of our long spears.
above us, the moon stood in watch.

there were never enough words
associating the badger with the fish
whom we prayed to.

the files made the barbs shine.
in our minds we imagined our spears
digging into his furry neck,
turning the snow and ice red
before its essence reached the ground.

she spoke of the vagueness
in her vision. the animals who
would benefit from this deed.
she sighed with relief and she forgot
what she was talking about when she found
i had already filled the bags and containers
with food and water.
medicine for our enervated bodies.

the clock on the wall ticked
and the blanket which was spread out
on the coarse floor made us close our eyes
and we saw pastures filled with apple trees.

the crow-colored man in the green shirt
surprised us when he quickly drew open
the curtains.

the sunlight entered the room in sequences.
i saw the wide-faced man
tearing open the breast of a bird.

he placed its lung on a white handkerchief
and he smeared his face with it.
i saw the tension of his life
on his face recede.
knots of human skin unraveled itself.

he spoke:
the sound of waves on a grey and misty
afternoon is but a fragment
and the pebble which i valued
because it came from the ocean
probably rolls behind me
whenever i walk by drunk
looking for the billfold
it was in.

the rotting flesh of the seal
and the damp sand on the beach
are better thoughts.

for whatever i was worth
and because i heeded instruction,
i released what i brought
in my palm.

parts of my life,
parts of everyone's life,

floated away in the foam,
the spit, the regurgitation,
the rebirth of fish.

this is what i gave,
this is what i am.

no one knows the reason why.
no one can ever do anything about it.
it's a long hallway with rooms
filled with dead friends.
the noise of their talking
grows quiet every time
you take a step.

if you persist
you will eventually learn
how to do the right things.

there used to be a path
into the lavender hills where we lived.
in someone's death, i was witness
to the unrecognizable beings who raised me.

i used to see a man comprised of white smoke
and he would take the billfold from his
pocket and i found myself doing the same.

whatever was in those billfolds
radiated.

in the morning i would hear of the man
who died from a hole in his back.
no explanation from anyone.
all the doctor said about him
led to alcohol,
the bottles that were scattered
around him.

i found the pebble beside

a rotting seal.
i thought to myself:
this is where it ends,
where the ocean begins.
this will be the farthest i will ever walk
to all those behind me who can tell me who
i am, where i fit among them.

i see my life collect itself on the foam.
my family drifts by.
my mother and father drilling holes
in the maple tree, my sisters and brothers
carrying silver buckets of sweetwater,
my uncles standing next to each other
huddled over the buzzing chain saw.

i place the pebble in my billfold.
i hear people behind me.
seagulls walk frantically down the path.

the door opened into the bright
moonlight.
the man in the white smoke
stood with his arms gesturing
towards the west.

bubbles collected in the foam,
in old bandages and photographs,
in a pink wooden leg.
i remembered the brown skin of the stout
puffy-eyed man. he would smile in the blue-green
summer air. we danced and stomped with our chests
out and we called out to him in the voices
of grown men. he smiled at us again when we
went back to our young laughs.
greasy fingers, the taste of strawberries
and watermelon.

like a person representing acclimation.
like being somebody to remind somebody
of the tubes in my body,

the expanding of my chest
and my legs hopping through
the daylight in remembrance of a song,
of a people in charcoal,
in dance.

there were times when i realized
after the colors changed on the floor
that the sun was out warming the earth
with its light and that hours earlier,
it passed through the bodies
of all those who knew me,
all those whose names
i brought to the ocean.

i bowed my head among a thousand seats,
facing the gradually appearing snowcapped
mountains in the north.

men in white clothes drove by
on small machines cutting the grass.
all day in bed i thought it was important
that i had been the first one
to walk across the freshly cut lawn.
it was important to know that my dewy tracks
led away from my despair
of always needing someone
around me
to console me
whenever i near the point
where it seems i'll forget my gift
to the ocean.

THE BIRDS ARE HOUSED IN A SMALL GLASS HOUSE

the birds are housed in a small glass house
and as they eat nonstop
the food disappears

reflections of their fat bellies amuse them
they inspect their fluffy bodies
and i can see they are content
to be trapped inside

below us, the chained dog walks nervously
no school kids to greet and pet him on saturdays
but the ones who do walk by
ignore him and like an asshole begging
for money or a drink
the dog named chilly willy
barks for attention

winos emerge from an alley in los angeles
near chinatown panhandling for dimes
we have but cheese and bread
they accept

the winter for the maladjusted kids has brought
on a new interest instead of staying home
in front of a television set
they now take pains
in their whiteness to explore the wilderness
which sits beside the frozen creek
which runs behind the apartments
and out into the football field
inside the living room i place the squirrel's
head within the crosshairs of a telescopic sight
he goes about within his morning
climbing out to the last dried buds
of the maple tree

i see my slippery fingers
prying open the boiled skull of the squirrel
the delicious beige lines of his brain
rare indian caviar
the trees gently rock and the obese squirrel
relaxes by stretching across a limb
he has stopped the electricity
the kids talk louder and the ice crumbles
under their weight

the other grey birds on the branches cleaned
their feathers as if it was an act
of establishing their boundaries

they sharpened their beaks until they saw the glimmer
of a sun hovering above them in the clouds

there was one blind bird who trotted over
the branches
memorizing each configuration

in the field near by, silhouettes of dashing rabbits
streaked through the dense brush
on the rooftops of the neighborhood
smoke appeared to climb back into the chimneys
flakes of snow gathered on the window sill

i sometimes wonder what we are doing here
living next to all these white people on this hill
it doesn't make sense when you hardly know
anyone and when you do know someone
it's a person who's trying to place him
and yourself into definition
into a role

overall, nothing helps anyone's search

i dream of a kind lady dressed in ironed
clothes and her shiny black hair
rushes by the many rooms of our thoughts

she walks into some when we are sleeping
she can't help herself
too many thoughts
in one house

on a parched mint-green stationery
i am fond of the poem sent to me
written by luyu
of rain-drenched mountains
excited neighbors

i see her by the window and she thanks the *one*
who delivered the snow
she compares the pitch-black night
to the nights of winter with the light
from the snow illuminating
whatever was visible

the occupants of the house sometimes questioned
themselves in the morning as to whether or not
they heard sounds of someone leaning over their beds
the two younger brothers blamed alcohol
one girl thought it had to do with the baby
she lost years before
the father of the girl looked at himself
in the mirror and he cursed the clan
of her daughter's husband

the painted baskets on the wall
along with the egyptian hanging vibrated
to the warm breeze of the heater

i sketched out a picture of a man
the room of his mobile home had broken windows
glass was lying all around the floor
and he had a gun pointed to his foot
after all this time
he had just learned he was just
as different as his wife was
but more bone-like

i had no way of telling he was drunk
and delirious
i had no way of telling of the gentle fawn
who would nurse his wounds
listen to his lies

in whose memory do we see a young man fighting
his mother

his uncles helped him hide his whereabouts
there was a girl in blue ski pants
washing dishes and her glasses were shaped
like butterflies
she stepped back when the fighting began
the vision of a dying rabbit
struggling within its own blood in the snow
flashed vividly in her mind

how do we catch this and hold it

later explain how we came upon the crossing
of our lives

i value the obsession with tranquil colors
and the damp smell of the spring wind
the helpless souls and the sound of crickets
and the moonlight which absorbs all our actions
all of our pain and decadence

he is each person from each season
with different faces of denial and rejection
the design of yellow pears on the curtains
will fade in the constant sunlight
it makes sense to remain inside
to think of it as being necessary
to sit here on this chair
watching the automobile smoke
spiral up past the trees

like a snake the wind picks up

the snow and swirls it around our windows
icicles plunge to the ground

as the hours pass in this day
mist covers the glass
the frozen earth
the frozen snake

we are held in suspension like the life
forms under the earth in the mud

we are under the constant resolution that
we have overcome all obstacles of learning
nothing else is hidden
by simplicity and by spirit

whatever argument we have for living
has been set aside by those who truly believe
in the capability of the mind
to make it possible to carry on
with the act of recollection

the dark shell which covers us
is a resting eyelid

and we are in its liquid
we tell each other of the time gone by
most of us have no purpose although we are encouraged
to think so

I CAN STILL PICTURE THE CARIBOU

how far away from death do we imagine ourselves
to be?
is it something to be thought of
from day to day
like the portrayals of lives
on television that people watch,
filling their monotonous and dreary lives?
when my time comes
for participation in anything,
i sense that i will be in a confined state
of mental illness. a lost soul.
an animal who runs back and forth
over the beach,
desperately missing the scent
and the shadows of the people who raised him.
a mental block of my absolute helplessness.
the trouble with me is,
i can't go on pretending
nothing else is needed
to back up your character,
your presence, anywhere.
i have grown into a world
of people pointing and accusing
other people of each other's incompetence
and uselessness.

i am the angle of a secluded corner,
of a closet, of light
disappearing into light.
through my life ahead,
i picture surgeons
standing around me.
we have asked them if there will be complications
with your one lung.
they told us they can't tell us anymore.
go ask again just to see they're not lying.
they said the same thing again.
the coarse paint on the wall
divides itself into another shade.

white and black electric cords
pulsate under the sunlight on the floor.
silver knobs sit on various machines.
the suited man on television talks
about the need to preserve alaska.
caribou migrations. salmon and the brown bear.
mated eagles in the snowfall.
let's save the f-ing things.
they're comparable to the migrations
of the wildebeest in africa.
when it finally came
to the point of closing the curtains,
one of the doctors came in
and asked me if it was all right
for them to throw away my lung
like garbage.

as the sun was going down, the red car
raced through the stone-smooth highways
of the endless farmland.
patches of snow regathered the cold
from the shadows in the ditches.
the low rumble of the mufflers
grew quiet as the car passed over
the iron bridge.
below them, the frozen river
ran through the passengers' lives
like thoughts.
like a syringe collecting
blood. our mind. this open wound.
out from the clouds,
though invisible, there are vines
as thick as tree trunks,
coming down from the sky,
entangling us.
this is how we sometimes
know where we are being led to.
the people you meet are accidents.
we like to think
otherwise.
once those tree trunks found
the three of us passed out

in a junked car.
it was the middle of january
and when we woke we arranged our bodies
as if we were going for a ride.

seventy-five years ago, our places
were probably filled with dance
and constant prayer.
breath made of the day's
offering instead of alcohol.
alcohol made us dream of the car's
green interior lights.
the surgeons may keep their secrets
as long as the one lung keeps me.
let it be so important to them.
to the west, the animal
has stood on its hindlegs,
exhausting himself,
looking for something which will eventually
be lost.
the beach is dotted with his chaotic tracks.
the polluted seagull flies out from the waves
over the rolling ocean.
his feathers are packed together.
his imagination is as good
as anyone's.
he dreams of a swim
into the curling waves.
telephone calls bring police
to the ten tons of weapons
we buried.
we listen for stories
and read papers, novels, but everything ends
up the same, either dead, barely living,
or else there are senseless men with clubs
killing off the young harp seals,
the porpoise.
it started with the buffalo
and now because hunters shoot too much
caribou, wolves are shot from helicopters.
in the white man's own stupidity,
bear is still hunted in montana.

of course, nothing is new.
the actors within all of us keep us going.
the animals have no actors.
tuna fleets have been suspended
for two months. they think this will solve
the problem of the porpoise.
we walk into a room and we listen
to the educated man talk about his paranoia
of eventually living until his grandchildren
no longer resemble his race.
the world will consist of grey people
with grey gods.
many will try to revert.
they will choose any origin.
death will be anybody's choice.
if a baby is asked whether he chooses
life or death, there must always be someone
present to represent the baby.
the symbol that we will live by
will be a legless and headless man.
paintings and collages will always express
the desires of simplicity.
windowless houses and buildings.
no mirrors, glass, or refractions.
work and food will be small.
no mention of pay or anything
financial.
because one of us cared enough
not to see the other suffer
through comparisons,
one of us left.
my call out to the hallway
went unanswered.

the eventual death of the animal on the beach
made us aware of each other's
capabilities.
i was one of the carpenters' helpers
sweating in the lush green valley.
the rushing water from the creek
sometimes sounded like dishes
banging against each other.

dust from the passing cars
and trucks settled over our eyebrows.
someone said something about meat decaying
and the sound of hammers started over again.
the fat man in overalls carefully
tape-measured the length
of the room and he paid particular
attention to the dimensions
of the four corners.
he scribbled out his equations
on the pinewood.
grey river birds honked through
the treetops.
the red sun found us thinking
over the thoughts that once slowed
our lives. the young seal's coat shimmers
under the neon lights of new york.
i am disappointed at how many people
are killed by the great white shark.
there should be more.
red triangles within the chest cavity.
there's no special reason.
it's just an unwanted day.
the red car returns over the bridge.
and the call i made out to the hallway visibly
turns into small black letterings.
in the sleep and darkness of my skull,
i can still picture the caribou,
running alongside a green moist hill
with its antlers raised up towards the sky.
with clouds everywhere.

AFTER THE FOURTH AUTUMN

for e

it
like almost any
other anachronism
in my existence
is a test
and on the sides
are people
curious
on finding out
how and when i'll die
we pretend we're
related
and that when
we hear of the young
sister's disapproval
of the baby
melissa
i resolve
the bitch in
question
grew promiscuous
long before us
she will never surpass
or outgrow her
woman things

FOR THE RAIN IN MARCH: THE
BLACKENED HEARTS OF HERONS

i see myself sleeping
and i see other ignorant people
locked securely in their houses
sleeping
unaware of the soft dawn-lit
furbearing animals
wrapping themselves with the bark
and cone from pinetrees
within each of their thoughts
there is the vision
of the small muskrat's
clasped hands
the struggling
black and yellow
spotted body of a salamander
freeing itself from a young
girl's womb
in my dark blue pickup
i came upon a cigar-smoking
badger
who invited himself and
later came to my home
gathering chips and splinters
of my firewood and starting
a fire
for an hour we sat
and then he suddenly stood
on his hindlegs and walked
over to the stove
and opened it
he took out two narrow pieces
of burning wood and rammed them
into his eyes
he fell on all fours
and then made rumbling sounds
mocking my pickup with its two
dull headlights

disappearing into
the forest

i dream of a painter
in the desert who tells me
his twisted and contorted
paintings of indians
amuse him because it's
the type of stuff whites buy
and enjoy
how i guess they still see us
because his family once helped
the spaniards build missions
in california
at least he knew his parents
were indians
that's what the old man
in the field kept telling us
flower petals crumbled through
his fingers
but we already know how the cycle
goes
the trees and the weeds
quickly grow and decay
in the reflection
of his sunglasses
his lips and teeth are still
stained with coffee and tobacco
the cross-eyed boy
smirked at his remarks
he was impressed
with the mountains anyway
not the seeds that went into
the earth
not with the man-sized fish
who waited each spring
for the river ice
to break up
to feed on the offerings
of miscarriages
he was told and experienced
all in one night

somewhere in canada
the cactus and the medicine
they called peyote
deep inside that night
he thought he knew and he probably
sat through the whole two-day ride
back to chicago thinking he was
truly indian
he probably thought it
right up until the moment
he pissed and examined
his shriveled body
in the showers
seeing and feeling for the last time
the bitter green liquid

within each of our lives
as we are growing we are given
and we experience these choices
but it isn't until later after we have
filled ourselves with bowls and bowls
of another food that we realize we have
chosen the wrong side
i know it will be the same for me
for there was a time last week
when i forgot to bring alive
into someone's mind
a hand reaching into hot boiling
water
a ball of fire bouncing
in front of the yard
in my childhood i can remember
what it felt like to feel the power
and mass of a ship i later recognized
as a spanish galleon
everytime i vomited into
the light-green lard can
i saw the underside of this
ship
sailing past the man who
called to me
he sat back against the black

cardboard wall and whenever he smiled
i could see his coarse white hair
his yellow fingernails

the next time i saw him
a bald-headed hooked-nosed man
in overalls stood in the brilliance
of the summer daylight
the bright green grass reflected
on the linen and the dishes shined
and the aroma of chicken and corn
filled the nostrils of people
and the mangy dogs who were my pets
watched from under the porch
he will stand in the place
of your grandfather
your grandfather will watch
this day pass through
his eyes
years later he sometimes waved
to me on the road as he drove back
from his soybean fields
he would stand on his tractor
i never knew what he said to me
that one day under the apple tree
when he stood in replacement
of my grandfather
i was too busy thinking
about the middle-aged man
who lifted up the sleeping girl's
dress that morning:
he was laughing but it sounded
more like grunting
i had just woke and it seemed
like he had been standing over the girl
waiting for me to open my eyes
because the blankets had been moved
to one side of her
he pointed under the dress
he touched and then he clowned and mimicked
and then hobbled out of the house
with a barrel of dishes

from then on whenever i saw him
he did his clown act which always
left me humored
but i will never forget one fall night
ten years ago when the sound of a pheasant
brought us together
through his song i watched
the day and night split in half
inside the electric lightbulb
and through each motion
of my mind and body
i saw a birchtree give birth
to snowflakes
there was a horse
and then a man
they each divided portions
of themselves and then they walked
away as one
the next day without any night's rest
i chopped wood for my grandmother
all afternoon
i imagined the wood as being things
i wanted to go rapidly behind me
there was no room for the mother
who shot her son in the neck
no room for the man who said
he'd pull the trigger on the lives
of six people
all lined up in a row
unless it was completely understood
why he came back

through the screen over the opened
window i felt the small hands
of a toad examining my round
face
the hammock moved within
the toad's breath and when he
walked away boils grew over the places
where it had touched me
it was later explained to me
that i was born the same moment

a baby strangled on its own cord
several miles away
so now whenever i stand in front
of a mirror
i go over the small star-shaped
scars
and tell myself that i will
always be afraid of all those born
before me
i listen for the whippoorwill
directing dwarfs to the place
where they will find cigarette butts
the rubber tires of the automobiles
crunch against the rocks
on the road
through the rubble of the fire
of the old blind man's house
all they found was his pink
wooden leg

my mother spilled a box of bullets
on the table
she placed one into an empty coffee can
and poured several capfuls
of grey ash into it
from the window
sparks and the retort of the rifle
spiraled into the blackened hearts
of herons
we looked into the forest
and we saw the silhouette of a pickup
the occasional dim red glow
of someone smoking
it was us in our life ahead
i will never know who i actually am
nor will the woman who lives with me
know me or herself or the children
we want
i am always surprised at how many
different minds drift across
each other
some resenting everyone

some imitating what they will
never be
others make room for others
and then there are us
afraid of everyone because they
are afraid of us
unable to fit anywhere
although we live in apartments
we take weekend drives and visits
to our land with the idea
of getting away from our frustrations
we find ourselves confronted
because of our unity
sisters and aunts blab
within their drinks
when we enter the skidrow taverns
as if they had sat in complete boredom
with nothing to discuss
until they saw us
ordering a couple of beers
from the corner in the dark
restoring everyone's indignation
towards us
we shrug our shoulders
thinking it isn't as bad as trying
to outstare the whites all weekend
but it is
rednecks press their fat longhaired
faces against the window counting us
and i reach into my coat
setting my pistol's safety catch
into fire
it is their daily fantasy
while pouring cement into foundations
or else while scattering cowshit over
the fields of their fathers
to think of themselves finally
secluding me and beating me with their fists
and it is my fantasy to find myself
cornered by four of them
to see the sparks
of my automatic

flashing under their hairy bellies
sirens of police cars and ambulances
whine through the brick alley
they question me
and i tell them it was self-defense
a story they never believe or get tired
of hearing
but the big redhead thinks different
i knew these boys
they wouldn't jump anyone
he turns around and i place
the cold barrel of his .38
behind his pink ear
i squeeze the trigger
and the brain explodes
and splatters everywhere
on the white panel of the ambulance
i create the design and the painting
of his life
i walk away from the wet black streets
of the country town
thinking of my painting
the salamander spearfishing
in the coldest day of winter
for dead fish

coming back i read the poem pow-wow
written by w. d. snodgrass after
visiting my people's annual tribal
celebration
you can't get away from people
who think what they see
is in actuality all they will
ever see
as if all in one moment they can sense
automatically what makes a people
what capabilities they have of
knowledge and intellect
he was only shown what was allowed
to be shown
what the hell did he expect
out of his admission fee?

and as far as he thinking that he knew
more about indians than they themselves did
he should have thought twice
it's the same way with the poem
i am a sioux brave, he said in minneapolis
by james wright and countless others
he will never know the meanings
of the songs he heard
nor will he ever know that these
songs were being sung long before
his grandfathers had notions
of riding across the ocean
long before translators
and imitators came
some claiming to be at least a good 64th
grabbing and printing anything
in scrapbook form
dedicating poems to the indian's loss
writing words and placing themselves
within various animals they knew nothing of
snodgrass will never know what spirit
was contained in that day he sat above
the feathered indians
eating his hot dog

he saw my people in one afternoon
performing and enjoying themselves
i have lived there 26 years and although
i realize within my life i am incomplete
i know for a fact that my people's ways
aren't based on grade-b movies
and i also know that the only thing
he will ever experience in life
as being phenomenal
will be his lust
stirring and feebly coming alive
at the thought of women
crumbs from the bread
of his hot dog
being carried away
by images of crushed
insects

my father speaks to us
as we sit in the living room
he is in the other room
sketching in detail the face of his father
he'll be there for several days
and we won't see him
we have gone back for the weekend
again
nothing changes
there's not much i can say
to the indian who beats other indians
he lives in his long trailer thinking
he has finally settled into
the land he hardly knows
thinking he will forever
be a man even if my brother and i
make his face bruised and swollen
nothing seeps into people like him
sitting here i can see
his teethmarks on my knuckles
and he has vowed to me
the only thing which will separate us
is death
between coming here to this desk
and going outside this apartment
for fresh air
i spend my time throwing my fists
in rapid succession toward the mirror
i have always been confident with myself
ever since i entered the boxing ring
in des moines years ago
i used to think i was an asshole
stepping into the canvas and now it's
no different
i am training for a fistfight
which will be fought in an alley
or out on some country road
against a drunk whose honor
i offended
i didn't make it easy for my father
as my grandmother had told me to
friday night

leave your ill feelings outside
the house
or else you will disturb
or push against him
what he is looking for
while my sisters take turns
combing my mother's hair
we hear him talking within
his room shelling kidney beans
we are with him on his walk
through the fog with wilbur
his nephew
checking the traps along
the river
on the way back they see a young
dismembered body of a girl
scattered for a quarter of a mile
they do not talk to each other
through the whole stretch
of the railroad tracks

a man comes to us
and he greets us and we exchange
kind words with him but we are puzzled
when we find after he has left
that we are still thinking about him
i place a hand in my pocket
and i touch and feel one single bean
for an evening we sit
trying to figure out how
the man placed it there
for each block and section
of color or a shade which
comes close to it
he divides them into several
of the more luminescent ones
the black paint of the tempera
outlines our features
shadows are layers of color
going from darkest to lightest
dead fish pile on top

of one another and the snow
continues towards spring
before the frogs sing
furry-shaped men light their fires
as they wake in their caves
a handsome man paddles by in his boat
and the three women on the shore
of the river frantically wave their arms
to him but he ignores them and he goes
downriver
he is bothered by the thought
of flashing minerals
dates and calendars
how the times remind
him of *the russian
messenger*

MARCH TWENTY-EIGHT/1977

my finger is still numb
and it's been five days now since
for no reason it started to swell
and upon our observance it twisted
and touching it
one could hear and feel
the crunching of small delicate bones
when i went to
the next room to show it
to someone other than
my wife, it took its
normal shape
no discoloration
that next morning we went
to the ditch behind the mailbox
where my hand searched the ground
for our cigarettes
we saw the young plant there
standing on the exact spot
where we thought it would be
my finger could have brushed
against it
or else its essence
was extracted by the incorporeal
and that what happened was supposed
to happen
the two dogs who visited us
the transformation of a giant rabbit
hopping a hundred yards
with wings surfacing on its back
lifting its bird body
to the night on its last hop
whatever is growing now over
the earth
there is so much strength behind it
i see it as a counteracting force
between the points of two knives
knowing that when one slips
it will go through my heart

POEM ONE

it begins with the unfolding vision
of a man swinging his head and neck
like a chicken swallowing water
convulsively
the perfect regurgitation
of a copper tube
how it formed an o
as it came up
in his mouth
before he took it in his hands
rolling and cupping it
singing and spitting upon it
sewing with it like a needle
through canvas through
the patient's knee

when it was time to sleep
i turned the blankets over
to lie down but it was interrupted
by beads of cold water that i felt
on my left shoulder
earlier a garbage bag
collapsed by itself

fifty miles south
a fire appeared across a stream
by my relative's house
a hand touched the screen
farther south
it was associated that
the recent brother who hung
himself in an oklahoman jail
was in effect lonely for the unexplained
hanging of his brother who was home
on leave from the marines
relatives had been outside and below
the walls of his cell window
it was said that voices

were heard in english
voices that weren't supposed
to be there
he was a singer who i thought
was a part of who i wanted
around me to listen to
and now since i know he was death
i trudge behind him
perplexed when bruises appear
over his suicidal face

even though our vision was limited
we could see into the ground fog
and haze above us
we stood hoping the geese
would come towards our way
as soon as they appeared
i let out a shout
and they swerved northward
we started firing our rifles
we knew it was too far

later as we walked on
i regretted firing upon them
it was stupid
immediately i thought
of the pistol i carried inside
the compartment of the nova
ever since pickups started
chasing me on highways
and mainstreets
it was strictly there
to defend us
i didn't know what comparisons
to make and resolve due to my
feelings of respect for the geese
my dependence on the pistol

there were the human-colored feet
of silver squirrels
that later hung on our belts

in the sunlight
i carefully observe
the grey-blue fog in your eyes
along the border of your pupil
the mechanic-like instrument
the dotted purveyor and restorer
of our daily encompassment

it isn't known yet whether
there is a cure for the deafness
in my brother's left ear

both men who can "see"
have verified the cause
attributed to the accidental
brush against menstruation
by the cup used
or the mouth kissed

she wishes for someone to leave
the innards for the owl outside
perhaps it's just hungry
i am thinking it's probably why
he comes each night
the summer is gone anyway
sheets of ice have formed
over the stream and along
the rims of the puddles
on our driveway
laborious insects tunnel their way
deeper into the dead trees
they are similar to spirits
retreating for the winter
their arms are retracted
except for the one finger
which searches about
feeling for signs of frost
scratching the dirt
taking in only enough
to cover them

HAVING DRAGGED THE SHELL
OF MY HOUSE

it wouldn't make sense to anyone anyway
so i figure there's no use trying
to impair someone's daily monotony
by recording mine

i haven't felt it much
the only thing i want is for things
to go well
and for me to confess
to the one who'll see
if there is anything wrong
w/me

i observe the red white-eared deer
standing under the sunflowers
i sense women locked
in confrontation
she
in her soiled clothes
her words are hate
for my protégé
who wears a wig
a persistent target
of physical attacks

it wasn't because of her
hitting her
it was because the other one
mistook that she was being
challenged
actually your sister was doing motions
of her head and hands emulating
the antics of a psychopath

hopefully we listen to the same songs
on the radio

a precarious judgment
for a day which in our thoughts
has begun a seed of our reflections

as i blink my eyes twice
this spring
two humans pass into the world
of death several miles
apart on a highway

the leftover food in the garbage
bags moves by itself
chimes ring inside the plaster
wall

the painting of a brown oval-faced
girl came out from the closet
and it now sits under the table

the green wind of the trees
in the sunlight shines through
the teapots and the fruit

small birds swerve their bodies
in between the chained barking dog
and the tangle of black electric wires

POEM FOR NOVEMBER

first there is the natural
but from this: who & how many can actually
touch
the traveling desolate
speck of dust
representing someone's
path
when we believe it
to be an act of rebirth
which exists in chosen blood only, otherwise
it is memory
an abandoned shadow
casting its last imprint
over us
or a call
from another spectrum where
i am the earth
resulting in warped
generations from
a seal's anxiety in a circus
to swim on a hot
summer day combined with
an unintentional stare at a funeral
descended through
the fiber and tissue
of our developing womb & left us
a dent in our ears and lips
incredulous and reticent
with nothing to sustain even the ordinary
and the times
when i am fortunate
enough to reaffirm
my hands and request
into a distant lucid spark
of two rocks
igniting a dry nest
the blind
pigmentless salamander
knows i am close
to seeing

POEM FOR DECEMBER

you know we keep coming
across one another
even though we give
the impression
people other than ourselves
can't exist
because of our tribal names
who is and isn't related to us
what harm or influence
you have brought
upon someone
that at times you hear
the high-pitched drone
in your ear
just how much you
understand of yourself
tests are given
common humans who share
the isolation of this
daylight
judge the eligibility
of my chances after death
many people utter my name
in disgust
hopefully some are in favor
of the indian vet
who calls himself a man
who i keep having encounters with
through the radio he receives
the message
he sees me as the viet cong
send the word up ahead
look it up in
flashback: regression of self
i'm supposed to be dead

POEM TWO/RAINBOW

what remains is the singular black man
sitting in his curtain-
drawn room
quiet and unchanged
even though i have disturbed
his gaze into the lights and dials
of his stereo
i only know him because he has offered
to translate my poems en español
i call my adviser who is his teacher
and he says
"i'd hold back on this if you're
considering publishing
i'd get someone who's sensitive
with the language"
but it was only a deal to help him
with his grade
as a result of his query
on the origins of my camouflage coat
he starts talking:
search and destroy
that was our task
sharpshooter for the tanks
i put 50 slugs in this one cat man
i am murietta
you mean you were in nam?
how old are you?
22?
and you were in the marines?
two years? 74 and 76?
he gets frustrated because i doubt
him
i try to resolve the matter
by rationalizing that acquaintances
died there too
that when my lottery number
came up in 69
i was surprised but a physical
reduced my chances of going 100%

didn't tell him of the times
i sat banging my bony fists
into my knee
seven years after surgery
i ask him about the button
which he gave me the other day
which i promptly refused
after seeing it inside the baggy
soft
fresh and moist with its liquid
dark chalky green
patterns of islands
entrapment
even through the plastic

i told him i only consumed
dry stuff
he laughed and asked if i ever
smoked it
i told him yes
how did it feel?
i felt mostly out of place
he laughed again
that was yesterday evening
the cactus is drying by the window
webs of cottony strychnine
my chapped hands are chilled
from the november wind
in his eyes he has the look
as if he had just extricated himself from
a woman
i'm sorry i came in
all i wanted was a nickel
thanks for the cigarette
anyway

THREE REASONS FOR TRANSGRESSION: THE FIERCE HEAD OF THE EAGLE, THE OTTER, AND THE DAYLIGHT

1.

i have lost you completely now
nothing brings back memory
of you or of me having anything
to do with you
we keep hearing you scream
in your weekend drunkenness
that you don't give a shit
anymore
bored by your obsession
the other drunks
sensing impermanence
have no alternative
than to agree with you
they ride in packs
looking for me
having things turn around
on them
they found themselves
under our fists
don't ever contest me
in courts
you would lose
if i shot you
in front of your house
i would go free within
a month
no one would care
about the outcome
if i went and shot
the other half who's
just as crazy
i'd still go free
that in itself is strange

but it's true
the man who is walking
75 miles away
is testimony to this
lucky him
going to school
(anymore he isn't satisfied
to at least be able to walk
in the daylight to know he's left
behind sticks for what resembled
a son to his father
another son to whom he feeds
naming the name of the other
who floats by like a speck
of dust)
and me
i continually receive letters
from a big-assed white
informing me of the tribe's
depleted education funds
maybe so
but i perceive an indian
who has returned from failing
acculturation in the city
sticking it to her
telling her what to tell me
of how much time i am allotted
to complete school
i am unaffected
i hold readings and workshops
for subsistence
i try to refrain from several topics
as if an aura of magic
encompassed them
and with each word i would lose
parts of a sequence of thought
of an otter swimming and taking food
in its mouth to a dejected person
on a small sandy island
the buds on the trees outside
this apartment are light green
and the birds sing all night

and the air is filled
with the rapid movements
of earth and people
i feel i am growing stronger
whenever i stand in front
of them
what do you do when there is a man
who represents your dreams
who goes talking and appraising
his deeds
and for no reason he stops
and says something new
there is a chance
for those who want to learn
but not for those who feel it
hard and difficult
that's the way it's been for me
i leave alone the thought
of an old movie house
and we twitch our necks
to laughs that aren't there
when we look
listening to the tape recorder
last night
something brought back
the memory of lodge grass, montana
a tribal member who had married into
the people
focused his eyes on me
as he sat and sang with a drum
composed with unfamiliar faces
we were locked into four separate
social structures
we knew we didn't fit
no matter how much impression we gave
doesn't matter really
the fact is
today he'll be buried
the memory of him enlarged
like a photograph
twice last night
i never thought it was important

until i opened the papers
this morning to read his services
will be held today
i think i've got to let
the pet rabbit go
i've got to let myself go
my teeth are tired of chewing
the masking tape which bonds
and cages us
outside it's as if
the weather's acting in accord
but the green buds on the treetops
are alive
they think different
they're not in objection
they are glad
the brittle glass cup
filled with coffee speaks to me
when i touch it for a drink
and i immediately sense
i have no need for answers
i'll always accept myself

cedar falls: the spinster
in political science

2.

no matter where i have stood
and sat within the past three days
i keep getting headaches
there were times when i would walk
across the campus on a hot afternoon
with blood spurting from my nose
and i would gag on clots
trying to hold my composure
i nod my head and agree
with the lighting selene offers
i feel the strain in my eyes subside
i hear the chimes on the curtain bar ring

195

i'm tired of smoking
i'm tired of drinking
i'm nervous in front of company
or else i run out of goddamned things
to talk about
i have nothing in common with anyone
it confuses circumstances even more
when instructors mention that something
would be terribly wrong if in their excavations
they found a rusted computer among
the american indian
why a black thought it was racist
of the associations made as english
being a common bond of a polity
that the black said it wasn't
because he could communicate
with any indian by walking up
to one and saying how
of the little squinty-eyed man
whose karma was once spilled
on the eastern front in the form
of a german officer's blood
how this one particular person
knows someone in the dept. of the interior
who said *they* wouldn't waste their f-ing time
if they wanted to utilize indian lands
for resources
characters like these play rough
to keep minorities down
places like gordon, nebraska
dead naked indians in dancehalls
it doesn't say much for what
they're trying to teach me
we came home because of my headaches
it's saturday night
the coffee is boiling
it reminds me of the rain
that fell this evening
it reminds me of two people
uttering and questioning
a person's name
the pinetrees bend and twist

above them
they chose to forget the name
to walk out safely from the woods

he writes
i try to be unconcerned about
the black doe-fawn council's decision
to accept a city indian's application
for overseer
maybe i'm doing it all wrong
although i have told myself
if the possibility ever arose
my being asked to take the job
i would turn it down
because of my self-doubt
as to how i would do publicly
with my mind in complete bilingual
awareness
able to verbally construct an opinion
and to substantiate my decisions
with knowledge and truth
experience with the past
and the past previous
on the inside i have nothing
to support the individual i am
at least that's how i see
a leader to be
not a joker
not anyone who feels
he wants to "help" on the spur
of a moment
those are the kind who hide
in their houses or else the kind
who come back after living in the city
for 20 or 30 years
i should plan on living there
for a long time
instead of wasting my time
on the pretense of getting my degree
and if things are as they are now
i will have no trouble obtaining
any kind of position

my simple white restraintless being
will pay for itself
they'll probably even build
a house for me as they have done
for her as to the man
who gave her the job gave himself
a house did
doesn't matter how much indian
i try to be
fact is
i have a better chance
if i become a white or a wino
for two-thirds of my life

it doesn't hurt to criticize further
closer to our origins
if he feels we are incapable
of holding the job then reluctantly
i don't have much faith with them
although they probably believe otherwise
they have illusions that they can sit
and at will outthink and outwit
each white representative that comes along
bringing documents and explanations
showing them the government's ways
of finding propensities
and solutions
to build and make use of tribal land
they can't understand everything
if i am having trouble
they are the same
it's not a matter of who has better
mental capabilities or comprehension
or who is the self-made man
what power he has or thinks he has
truth is
some of us go through life
like the fierce head of an eagle
perpetually deceiving the other man
mentally constructing a death
an injury or a sway
in how we wish the future to turn

when he transgresses our accomplishments

even though the flood
made the serpent grateful
for the scores of young catfish
who frantically swam along the growth
of the river's edge
the serpent regretted the day ever starting
he would die with his mouth wide open
spines from the catfish protruded
through his skin and muscle
behind the base of his skull
the lodged catfish spoke to him
inside his throat:
i like to tell people when
they are making assholes
out of themselves
there was nothing in your blood
no reason for the world to begin
that said *you* should make decisions

within the past few days
whatever belongs to me
has tumbled and turned
insidious
and my feelings pour out
into the darkness
of my chest cavity
old habits return like a parasitical
shadow who left years ago
and now returns through the window
which it purposely left open
as we dream
we accidentally place our fingers
through our chest
and into our hearts
we touch and feel it
talking to us:
it's up to you to define
what your name is
whose body it once wound itself

around
i was fresh from the womb
i never made it a point
to hate anyone
i question the incineration
of human flesh
that's the difference
to have doubt

in the early hours of the morning
we remember bits of conversation
but the idea of it overwhelmed us
even though we didn't understand it
it had to do with a disposal of a human
it had already sided with us
by the time thunderheads
began to show through the dawn
to the north
my wife had just loaded the pistol

we heard the jingle of his keys
as he walked to his car trunk
the last time i saw him
he was sliding the bolt
of his carcano against the barrel
i saw the gold gleam
of the bullet casing
i grabbed the pistol from her hands
and i began firing just as soon
as he rounded the car
his rifle discharged
after four of my bullets
struck him in the chest and face
twigs from the thorn tree
fell into the river
i got off the car
and went over to his body
and asked him if he had any beer
i took what he had in the trunk
and whatever drunks and winos
he had in his car

were glad to ride along
with us

3.

when i think of the process you have
unnecessarily gone through
of bearing a child
i don't know how it feels
even though i have tried
to understand at depth
the category in which fools
like us fit

in the end
there is no difference
the child grows
we slobber and blurt out
his name through the foam
of the beer
our wine-spotted clothing
born through years of alcoholic vision
we argue what his indian name means
when the best times occurred
why it was essential with each
person met to foretell him
the time of your death
times when we woke in our houses
with the wind inside
the windows all busted
relatives who didn't belong to us
we pass from car window
to car window
a printed sheet for his
shivering body
his father can barely speak
to us but we are reluctant to take
the baby from his father
he tells us the car won't start
and we assure him by saying
that if we see his wife

in town we'll tell her
to hurry with the gas
as we drive off
we look into the rearview mirror
and we see the baby instinctively covering
himself with the sheet
later we see his mother
being led to a silver pickup
by three fluorescent-hatted farmers
chapped hands and palms lined
with pigshit
strong talk among the guts
of headless catfish

we ask ourselves
if in effect we are anywhere
close to where we're supposed to be
if in fact the concept of learning
has been worth it
if it isn't by genetics alone
that i go around
reading and teaching
what's left
and what i've absorbed
i tell the students
of sidewalks and factory-centered
towns
of the poison produced and distributed
by their white fathers
through the rivers
and waters
of the poison their babies
will suck through the breasts
of their mothers
no one cares to know
some of them will eventually
grow insecure whenever
their supposed dominance
is threatened
telephone calls will be made
policemen take punches at me
even after i tell them it was me

the pickups were chasing
it's inevitable
there was the time we stopped
at wall drug, south dakota
i have no objection
to the commercialized springwater
we drank there but i hate the memory
of how i drove for miles disgusted
with the deliberately placed clumps
of human hair in our hamburgers
some of which we had already eaten
it's strange to check each thing
we buy now because of impressions
left
so much for the badlands

naturally we think it's good
to be on the auspicious side
when we see people suffer around us
and we amuse ourselves
with news of their silly acts
children are thrown
from cliffs into
the ocean

i once drew a picture
of a girl in pencil
who had lived inside a small box
inside the closet of her parent's home
for fourteen years
it reminded me of a rotten frog
who had somehow lived through the night
with half its body spread over
the hot sunlit highway
moss from the swamps
entangled itself to the lower
exposed organs and fibrous tissues
assorted insects flew about
and the frog blinked at each
passing car

FROM MORNING STAR PRESS AND OTHER LETTERS: 1978

the irregular pigmentation
on her skin
is a sign
that a thunderbird
is assisting her

we exist
and for each ongoing moment
regardless of where we are
ageless guardians of all shapes
and dimensions
be they animals or spirits
of past humans
dieties
who are natural
in our blood
they are our sentinels
revolving around us
but what were they thinking
fifteen years ago
when i sat openmouthed
in a dentist's cushioned chair
when over the radio
was broadcast the prediction
of the world coming to an abrupt end
at 3:30
the next day

my mother and uncle comically
thought its revelation was the main reason
instead of the usual pains of tooth
extraction that i lay idle with tears
but discreetly i was glad for not
having to go out and chop
the wet firewood
even though that evening
taps by my diligent foundry-breath

father urged me to get off my ass
but an explanation savored
with the aroma of pork hocks
and potatoes
stopped his rationale

i heard the crunching
of his voracious jaws against his teeth
and he complimented in reluctance
the mist on the window from the warm tea
distant glaciers broke apart
a vulture having sculptured
the land with its wings and body
risking its once beautiful plumage
sat bewildered
thinking it would have been simpler
to have been the chickadee
females hear as they near their cycles
instead he could recite
the names of all serpents
and he was the first to sight his brother
approach from the east
the tip of the feather on its head
the sun

for nothing i know of
i didn't tell them the pains were real
it is for the exact purpose
i sit here
now a victim of the earth's
rotating axis
the inherent seasons
outside
the snow is blowing violently
it seems to sit still but it meanders
covering and recovering
our frosted automobiles
the sun warms us through its tinted
filter and i think that when
we were created he or they
took special care of designing

our eyes
like the edge of a roof over a house
the skin has grown over yours
the long hair grows on my hair now
i even go farther as to claim
i must have been disillusioned
somehow turning the beautiful
to its limits
i went and now live where i wanted to go
all too suddenly i destroy things
which are in essence
ongoing like for instance time
when i first encountered the mute
at my doorstep who conveyed
he was my brother and proceeded to draw
a square into the air in front of him
with his two fingers entitled *assuage her*
it didn't matter
i had grown overanxious
and when i visualized the two animations
which were in between them
i relinquished that i had been correct
in not going out to the night
to go through the trouble of ritual
a ritual which should have ended before
and now our faces have reversed themselves
i see you walking into night
while i walk past you into day

for what holds me together now
it comes without the foam
from the ocean
it resembles a dream of a seagull-faced man
scurrying down the path of a wooded hill
bringing news of the man
a neighbor
who died from unnatural causes
there were bullets blessed and laden
with the odor of herbs
they momentarily appeared on his palms
he said take discretion
symbolic stones

watch me walk by somewhere
intoxicated
i thought it was a severe case
of an unwashed face
but when i observed closely
he had been stumbling from house to house
announcing the first day of his fast
right in the middle of summer
instead of the appropriate winter
in his decrepit face i saw the bounced
reflection of the sunlight someone had sent
from the underbrush with a mirror
his transience was clear

a woman who once made love
to the starblanket-wrapped man spoke
of clubbing gophers and foxes
basing her strength within the adoration
of them
she sat in its season
its backfire is the prisoner
she relates to a pair
of hands whose time
from abstention
found themselves behind iron bars
they were seen the winter previous
going their way reverently to the river
and on each occasion
they would have a new blanket
wrapped around the beaded
scabbard
she desires for someone to leave
cow innards for the owl outside
perhaps it's just hungry
it's probably why he comes
each night
the summer is gone anyway
the night is a stone wall with a mural
of our reenactment
and the smiling mask
over the train's face
whizzes by empty in mechanical grace

the worst possible has retreated
but now i worry over what to her is
life
in return and for the mutuality
of her existence
she is asked and she consents
unhampered by the below zero
weather
to cook for the temporal people
who sit all night singing rhymes
bilingually
to the two-faced haloed ram
all day their eyes are glazed
with the brown fluid of cactus
the little girl will remember her name
and the mournful singing of happy birthday
being flicked as ashes
from a cigarette of corn husk
that later her father would die
driving through the rain
to have thought one's self protected
in the very substance
which made you knowledgeable
living on its impediment
diversity
unique yes but i question why they are unable
to cook for themselves
there was a time she stopped walking
and a carved wooden face constructed
from elm pine cottonwood hickory oak
maple and sycamore
was directly aligned with her face
readjusting
her earrings she concluded its purpose
was aesthetic
except for the inconsistent noises
from the dishes in their racks
her sleep had been virtually unbothered
and she felt at ease until
she entered her father's room
moccasined feet trampled across the ceiling
where she had just been

all the drawers to his dresser were open
his personal effects were in disarray
next
she heard the scraping of a dog's claws
resisting the forceful shove from the doorway
onto the kitchen floor

demented indians from the city flocked
to the carrion they left
self-injected
they held mundane meetings
discussed at length the importance
of refrigerating their lunches
acquiring larger mugs for their coffee
to jobs they didn't want
they sent out mimeographed newsletters
in one the ability to type and compute
was a prerequisite for a one-day office-cleaning
job
caucasian wives straggled along
they were satisfied with toothless alcoholics
affairs with men their husbands
once treated
the lesbians downstairs are listening
to man-music
one of them imitates the man-singing
tomorrow
they'll receive the oysters of a wild pig
by mail
reason: they have no respect for peace
in the frames of my film
i scrutinize in detail the black-eared
pig and its markings

yesterday evening i heard the cry
of an eagle flying by
it's incongruous to think of the mouse
who sleeps under the seats of our nova ss
he has gone on drunks with us
subsisting on drops from our chins
of sloe gin

later he is the mouse
to turn against us
making his death imperative
my relatives would take word
of his action to a *visitor*
and i would be late
blanketless
in talking to him
to learn the consequences of his communion
with the animal

MARCH EIGHT/1979

for the eagles it is as it should be,
circling high above the settlement's ridge,
the three of them a family,
bonded permanently by the child
who hasn't yet seen us,
driving to him below on top
of grandmother universe,
avoiding the slushy potholes,
intent on filming them.

the father, russell;
the mother, joann;
their red-faced son, elgin, *be ki ka me kwi,*
fresh to this world, the air,
the skylight.

i pray for him that we shall one day
meet and talk in mutual good health
and i to explain to him my incredible joy,
how my mixed depression was momentarily
quelled.

THE INVISIBLE MUSICIAN

THE SIGNIFICANCE OF
A WATER ANIMAL

Since then I was
the North.
Since then I was
the Northwind.
Since then I was nobody.
Since then I was alone.

The color of my black eyes
inside the color of King-
fisher's hunting eye
weakens me, but sunlight
glancing off the rocks
and vegetation strengthens me.
As my hands and fingertips
extend and meet,
they frame the serene
beauty of bubbles and grain —
once a summer rainpool.

A certain voice of *Reassurance*
tells me a story of a water animal
diving to make land available.
Next, from the Creator's
own heart and flesh
O ki ma was made:
the progeny of divine
leaders. And then
from the Red Earth
came the rest of us.

"To believe otherwise,"
as my grandmother tells me,
"or to simply be ignorant,
Belief and what we were given
to take care of,
is on the verge
of ending . . ."

THE PERSONIFICATION OF A NAME

Our geodesic dome-shaped lodge
redirects the drifting snow.

Above us, through the momentary
skylight, an immature eagle
stops in its turbulent flight
to gaze into our woodland
sanctuary.

Easily outstared, we rest our eyes
on the bright floor. He reminds us
further of his presence through
the shadow movement of his wings:

Portrait of a hunter
during first blizzard.

Black Eagle Child.

THE LANGUAGE OF WEATHER

The summer rain isn't here yet,
but I hear and see the approaching
shadow of its initial messenger:
Thunder.
The earth's bright horizon
sends a final sunbeam directly
toward me, skimming across the tops
of clouds and hilly woodland.
All in one moment, in spite
of my austerity, everything
is aligned: part-land, part-cloud,
part-sky, part-sun and part-self.
I am the only one to witness
this renascence.
Before darkness replaces the light
in my eyes, I meditate briefly
on the absence of religious
importunity; no acknowledgement
whatsoever for the Factors
which make my existence possible.
My parents, who are hurrying
to overturn the reddish-brown dirt
around the potato plants, begin to talk
above the rumbling din.
"Their mouths are opening.
See that everyone in the household
releases parts of ourselves
to our Grandfathers."
While raindrops begin to cool
my face and arms, lightning
breaks a faraway cottonwood
in half; small clouds of red
garden dust are kicked into
the frantic air by grasshoppers
in retreat.
I think of the time I stood
on this same spot years ago,
but it was under moonlight,
and I was watching this beautiful

electrical force dance above
another valley.
In the daylight distance,
a stray spirit whose guise
is a Whirlwind, spins and attempts
to communicate from its ethereal
loneliness.

THE LAST TIME THEY WERE HERE

In between the deafening locust-shrill
on the apple tree, the locusts pause
at their own noise and then
to a silent signal they drop down
to another leaf or branch,
stopping when the chorus
starts again.

The last time they were here
this is what I remember:

I see my grandfather kneeling before
rolls of our delicately-tied belongings.
He instructs, "It will always be important
as you travel in life to tie protection
as I have just done."

As we move without him now, I think
about my belongings, spread apart
in three different houses. No matter
how powerful my sinew star-symbols
over my writings, they are defenseless
without my actual presence.

THE REASON WHY I AM AFRAID EVEN THOUGH I AM A FISHERMAN

Who is there
to witness the ice
as it gradually forms itself
from the cold rock-hard banks
to the middle of the river?
Is the wind chill a factor?
Does the water at some point
negotiate and agree to stop
moving and become frozen?
When you do not know the answers
to these immediately you are afraid,
and to even think in this inquisitive
manner is contrary to the precept
that life is in everything.
Me, I am not a man;
I respect the river
for not knowing its secret,
for answers have nothing
to do with cause and occurrence.
It doesn't matter how early
I wake to see the sun shine
through the ice-fishing hole;
only the ice along
with my foolishness
decides when
to break.

THE SONG TAUGHT TO JOSEPH

I was born unto this snowy-red earth
with the aura and name of the Black Lynx.
When we simply think of each other,
night begins. My twin the Heron
is on a perpetual flight northward,
familiarizing himself with the landscape
of Afterlife, but he never gets there . . .
because the Missouri River descends
from the Northern Plains
into the Morning Star.

One certain thing though,
he sings the song of the fish
below him in the mirror
of Milky Way.

It goes:

In this confrontation,
the gills of the predator
overtakes me in daylight near home;
in this confrontation,
he hinders my progress with a cloud of mud he stirs.
Crying, I ask that I not feel each painful part
he takes, at least not until I can grasp
in the darkness the entrance
of home.

FROM THE SPOTTED NIGHT

In the blizzard
while chopping wood
the mystical whistler
beckons my attention.
Once there were longhouses
here. A village.
In the abrupt spring floods
swimmers retrieved our belief.
So their spirit remains.
From the spotted night
distant jets transform
into fireflies who float
towards me like incandescent
snowflakes.
The leather shirt
which is suspended
on a wire hanger
above the bed's headboard
is humanless; yet when one
stands outside the house,
the strenuous sounds
of dressers and boxes
being moved can be heard.
We believe someone wears
the shirt and rearranges
the heavy furniture,
although nothing
is actually changed.
Unlike the Plains Indian shirts
which repelled lead bullets,
ricocheting from them
in fiery sparks,
this shirt is the means;
this shirt *is* the bullet.

ALL STAR'S THANKSGIVING

At midnight
when we finally signalled for
and received permission
to go outside and relieve
ourselves, I stepped off
the porch onto a steep cliff.
Immediately, I dropped
to the ground for fear
I would tumble down
the mountainside.
"Get up," said Facepaint,
the trickster who brought
me to his relative's *amanita*
congregation.
"There are no mountains
in the Midwest," he added.
Later, after he got me upright,
we went back inside.
Comforted by people,
I sat back against
the log cabin wall
and closed my watery eyes.
Suddenly, I was sitting on
a tropical beach with my legs
in the vibrant surf. In the breeze
I felt the sun's warmth. I became
sleepy, and when my head sank
into the wall, I woke up.
I soon discovered that
my left leg was missing.
I truly thought I had
sacrificed it as a brake
on the mountainside.
My frantic inquiry
made a spectacle until
an old man directly across
from me theorized "the leg"
probably became numb under
my weight. When I looked,

it was there. But the missing
leg dream was a minor problem
compared to the disconcertion
of thinking oneself in a state
of religious purpose: bilingual
songs and cigarette-smoking
constellations.

EAGLE CROSSING, JULY 1975

Without Selene
he didn't know what to do.
As was the case with his grandfather,
he felt no recourse but to start
a sculpture-mask,
hollowing out
the dish at first,
and then carving the face
of the Big Footed One,
Me ma ki ka ta ta.
He saw himself
as this reclusive entity,
confined to wait for
the glacier-aided breeze
of a summer night.
There were frequent
dreams that she would soon
return to caress the areas
where his human arms
and legs once were;
her perfumed fingers
would come through
the cottonwood mask
and touch his closed eyes.
To him, the summer was simply
the odor of accidentally burnt
skin, filtering like snake newborn
through the oven racks.
He sat before warm, uneaten
t.v. dinners, and he paid
little heed to self-collapsing
trash bags.
No longer could he
remember the details
of crisp frosted mornings
when he unerringly invited
names of both enemy

and relative into
his offering of flint chips
and shavings from a black
antelope tine. From a silver
Spanish lancepoint, which served
as the body of the feather-fringed
pipe — a symbol of epic campaigns
and Flag Wars — he smoked this mixture
along with Friesland tobacco, and he
thought of the mythical hot sun region
where the-people-who-pulled-up-their-
ladders lived. He saw himself
as a god-like antelope dodging
musket balls before his death.
The crudely-shaped star felt cool
on his chest: Religion & Broken
Hearts, he recited, somewhere
high above the earth's backbone
in the month of Thunder Moon.
Postcard from a suicidal year.

THREE POEMS

1979

1.

The high uncut grass was covered
with a cool sheen of dew.
Grasshoppers sat quietly
in the shadows — oblivious
to the fact that the price
of gasoline was the reason
for their August bed
and comfort.
The sun was beginning
to filter and mix into
the new green-colored forest,
all of which made for a ritualistic
morning.
There was never any indication
as to what made the Nicotines
decide to gather frogs
from their yard for bait.
First, the wife would merely
suggest the catching of *tte kwa me kwa*
when the humidity decreased,
how in the bank-pole evening
they would throw out their lines,
sensing by the firm splash
over the river's depth that they
were about, just by that sound
alone.
Unconsciously, the husband
would bring out the bait bucket.
Together they would talk,
reassuring each other if
they could find at least six frogs
before the sun fully rose,
tomorrow would mean fried flathead,
boiled potatoes, wild onions,

and Canadian ale.
Further, it would be an opportunity
to set aside portions of their catch
to supplicate *those who have passed*,
implanting within themselves this doubt
and reverence for existence.

2.

Everything is arranged for us
when we arrive in the small Norwegian town
for the poetry reading. To welcome us,
they release the Styrofoam snow,
and restaurants list the food
we like in their menus:
spaghetti for Selene
and chili for me.
Although we whisper
to each other as to what
we should drink, the waiter
with extraordinary hearing
orders milk and Pepsi from
a distance. On our drive
to the cliffs where the ancient
glaciers supposedly stopped,
we observe Caucasians who dress
and act like Indians: three middle-
aged men sit on a car hood and drink
their whiskey in public; an old lady
walks to town in a strong, even pace.
Jokingly, I sometimes tell friends
they have white opposites, but when
I actually meet mine, it isn't comical.
But through him, we are here.
Contrary to what is written
on the dust jacket of his poems,
I have never seen Mikhail B.
on or near the tribal settlement.
To say you are *a part* is no easy
matter. Before I question other
people's lives, there is my own

to consider. Together we read
from our work. I am sure the freshman
students do not understand my life
as easily as his. However, they are
amused at my ms. rejections from
elite east coast publications
(anything east of the Mississippi),
and why I am beyond the listless primitive
who tracks the extinct wolf.
After classes, a bearded professor
invites us to his country house —
a remodeled mental institute.
During lunch, adopted Chinese
children dash in and the professor's
wife plunges a spoon of peanut butter
into their mouths. I suddenly realize
when I touch the Chinese girl's
warped head that this place isn't real,
that it was arranged in haste.
The Martians are fascinated
by the cutbead barrettes
on my wife's hair and I am
puzzled why they have invited us.

3.

Before graph paper existed,
you planned the first series of geometric
communiques.
Although I can't decipher
the signals or the code,
I know from having seen computers
there is something reaching me.
The Czechoslovakian cutbeads which decorate
the barrettes in your hair
flash synchronously
by the candlelight: U.F.O.
I discuss the plight
of the grasshopper who had chosen
me the day previous (on my way
to the university) to oblige

his planned suicide by jumping
onto my path.
In Indian I told him:
It's simple to end yourself,
but me, I am in the human snowdrift already
in need of permanent shelter, simple income
and some excitement.
Venison takes the space in my freezer;
otherwise, I would take you there
as a favor to let you sleep until
the Iowa River freezes over and lower you
on hook in exchange for prehistoric-
looking fish.

MESKWAKI LOVE SONG

Ne to bwa ka na,	My pipe,
bya te na ma wi ko;	hand it over to me;
ne to bwa ka na,	my pipe,
bya te na ma wi ko;	hand it over to me;
ne to bwa ka na,	my pipe,
bya te na ma wi ko.	hand it over to me.
Ne a ta be swa	I shall light and inhale
a ta ma	tobacco
tte ske si a	for the single woman.
Ne to bwa ka na,	My pipe,
bya te na ma wi ko.	hand it over to me.

EMILY DICKINSON, BISMARCK AND THE ROADRUNNER'S INQUIRY

I never thought for a moment
that it was simply an act of fondness
which prompted me to compose
and send these letters.
Surely into each I held
the same affection as when
we were together on a canoe
over Lake Agassiz in Manitoba,
paddling toward a moonlit fog
before we lost each other.

From this separation came
the Kingfisher, whose blue and white
colored bands on chest and neck
represent the lake-water and the fog.
But this insignia also stands
for permafrost and aridity:
two climate conditions
I could not live in.

It's necessary to keep your apparition
a secret: your bare shoulders,
your ruffled blouse, and the smooth
sounds of the violin you play
are the things which account
for this encomium for the Algonquin-
speaking goddess of beauty.

Like the caterpillar's toxin
that discourages predators,
I am addicted to food
which protects me,
camouflages me.
I would be out of place
in the tundra or desert,
hunting moose for its meat and hide,

tracking roadrunners for their feathers.

But our dialects are nearly the same!
Our Creation stories hopped out
from a nest of undigested bones,
overlooking the monolithic glaciers.
This is what we were supposed to have
seen before our glacial internment.
That time before the Missouri River
knew where to go.

My memory starts under the earth
where the Star-Descendant taught me
to place hot coals on my forearm.
"In the Afterlife, the scar tissue
will emit the glow of a firefly,
enabling one to expedite the rebirth
process. This light guides one's way
from Darkness."

The day I heard from you,
I accidently fell down the steps
of a steamboat and lost consciousness,
which was befitting because
there was little rationale
for the play (I had just watched
onboard) of a man who kept
trying to roll a stone uphill,
a stone which wanted to roll downhill.
I found myself whispering
"No business politicizing myth"
the moment I woke up.
Gradually, in the form of blood
words began to spill from
my injuries: Eagle feathers
1-2-3 & 4 on Pipestone.

I now keep vigil for silhouettes
of boats disappearing over
the arête horizon.
I keep seeing our correspondence

arrange itself chronologically,
only to set itself ablaze,
and the smoke turns to radiant
but stationary cloud-islands,
suspended on strings above
Mt. St. Helens, Mt. Hood
and Mt. Shasta: Sisters
of Apocalypse waiting
for Joseph's signal.
They tell me of your dissatisfaction
in my society where traffic signs
overshadow the philosophy
of being Insignificant.

It is no different
than living under a bridge in Texas
beside the Rio Grande.
Please accept advice from the blind
pigmentless Salamander
who considers his past an inurement.
"Perplexity should be expected,
especially when such a voyage
is imminent."

I want to keep you as the year
I first saw your tainted photograph,
preserved in an oval wooden frame
with thick convex glass,
opposite the introvert
you were supposed to be,
walking in from the rain,
a swan minus the rheumatism.

All of a sudden it is difficult
to draw and paint your face
with graphic clarity,
when the initial response is to alter
your age.
Automatically, the bright colors
of Chagall replace the intent.
When the Whirlwind returned

as a constellation,
we asked for cultural acquittance,
but when the reply appeared as herons
skimming along the updraft
of the homeland's ridge,
we asked again.
It was never appropriate.
We were disillusioned,
and our request became immune
to illness, misfortune and plain hate.
Or so we thought.

Contempt must have predetermined
our destiny.
To no avail I have attempted to
reconstruct the drifting halves
to side with me.
All that time and great waste.
Positive moon, negative sun.

Way before she began to blossom
into a flower capable of destroying
or healing, and even during times
she precariously engaged herself
to different visions,
I was already dependent upon her.
Whenever we were fortunate
to appear within each other's prisms,
studying and imploring our emissaries
beyond the stations
of our permanence,
I had no words to offer.

Mesmerized, she can only regret
and conform to the consequences
of an inebriate's rage
while I recede from her
a listless river
who would be glad
to cleanse and touch
the scar the third mutant-flower

made as it now burns and flourishes
in her arms.

I would go ahead and do this
without hint or indication
you would accept me,
                    Dear Emily.

THE SUIT OF A HAND

He is finally asleep,
but first his coma sent the Mysterious Rat
who knocked and left scratch marks
on our door. We thought a cure was being
offered. But that same night,
as a result of our inability
to decipher the Rat's spelling,
a crane swerved above us
on the highway. We knew then daylight
had been ceased, that the Being of Fire
seen jumping from the wreckage
was death.

Shadows of past lives —
his mother, father — called him.
Even the Negative Parrot tried.
Death is lonely — a dangerous spring,
it must have planned on saying.
I now return for you . . .

But the Parrot was weightless;
it couldn't enter the hospital
to personally observe my relative's
demise. The Parrot's "soul" is stuck
in the entrance where electricity
combined with the weight of flesh
and blood only opens the second door:
I strangled the fluorescent green bird
in the glass enclosure before it had
a chance to revert to its original human
shape. Gita, the Danish nurse, in an ultra-
white uniform approached and screamed,
"What the hell are you doing?"
I mistook her as an evil accomplice
and threw the asphyxiated bird
to her.

I feel trapped: like The Incorporeal Hand
which wears the suit of a human hand,
punching out to us violently from inside
an empty grocery bag. The abundance of food —
fruits and meats — has no deterring effect.
No regard for the holidays. The whole thing
reminds me of an Alfred Hitchcock movie.
I taste the wind with my antennaes
and regress at the sound of a crow's
masculine howl.

THE KING COBRA AS POLITICAL ASSASSIN

May 30, 1981

About two miles east of here
near the Iowa River bottom
there is a swampy thicket and inlet
where deer, fox and eagles
seem to congregate every autumn
without fail.
When I am hunting there
I always think:
if I were an eagle
bored by the agricultural
monotony of Midwestern landscape,
I would stop, too.
This morning I dreamt
of a little-used road going
from an overlooking hill down
into their divine sanctuary.
I tried to drive through
thinking it was a short cut
towards tribal homeland,
but stopped after the automobile
tires sank into the moist earth.
I walked down the ravine and met
two adolescents and inquired
if the rest of the road was intact
or passable. A bit wary of me
they indicated that they didn't
know. A faceless companion
rolled down the car window
and spoke in Indian.
"Forget them! They shouldn't
be here, anyway."
I walked on. Further down
I met a minister and began
to chat with him about
the tranquil scenery,

how far the road extended
into the land founded
by the Boy-Chief in 1856.
(I avoided the personal
question of whether the dense
timber reminded him of South America.)
He turned and pointed with his black arm
to a deteriorating church mission
in a distant valley.
"Yes," I said. "The Founder's wish —
when he purchased this land —
was a simple one."
Soon, a hippie with an exotic snake
wrapped decoratively around
his bare arms and shoulders joined
our polite and trivial
conversation about directions.
As we were talking the hippie
released his hyperactive pet.
We watched it briefly as it slithered
over the willows. We did not think
too much of the snake until it slid
towards a nearby stream,
stopping and raising its beady-eyed
head intermittently, aware of prey.
Following it, we discovered what held
its attention: a much larger snake
was lying still and cooling itself
in the water. I told the hippie,
"You better call your pet."
With a calm face he said,
"I'm not worried; watch
the dance of hunting motions."
And we did.
The larger water snake recoiled
into its defensive stance
as the smaller slid into
the water. Before each came within
striking distance, the hunter-snake
struck. They splashed violently
against the rocks and branches.
Decapitated, the water snake's

muscled body became lax
in the sunlit current.
I thought about this scene today
and the events which led to it
many times over, analyzing its
discordant symbolism.
I finally concluded this dream
had nothing to do with would-be
assassins, cinema-child prostitutes,
political decision-makers or anything
tangible. In *Journal of a Woodland Indian*
I wrote:
"It was a prophetic yearning
for real estate and investments;
something else, entirely . . ."

A DRIVE TO LONE RANGER

Everyone knows the Indian's existence is bleak.
In fact, there are people who have taken it upon
themselves to speak for us; to let the universe
know how we live, eat and think, but the Bumblebee —
an elder of the Black Eagle Child Nation —
thinks this sort of representation is repulsive.
This past winter, after our car conked out
in 80° below zero winds, we decided to pay him
our yearly visit. Although part of it was done
for amusement, we soon found out there were serious
things in life to consider. The poem which follows
was written without much revision. In fact, most
of it was composed in his earth lodge. I can still
remember the warmth of his antique woodstove,
as well as the silence after he shut off
his generator. He smiled at us as he accepted
a carton of Marlboro cigarettes.

For listening and instructional purposes,
the Bumblebee confesses that he sleeps
with earphones attached to his apian body.
"As the crisp December wind makes the constellations
more visible, so too, are the senses. Our vision
and hearing benefits from this natural
purification. Hence, the earphones."
In a lethargic tone someone offers
the standard "so they say" answer.
But the old man is unaffected,
and he continues to animate
what is in his Winter Mind.
"Ever since the Stabs Back clan
made the decision to accept education
for the tribal reserve in the late 1800s
there has always been an economic
depression. And now, when the very land
we stand on could reverse this congenital
inequity, the force which placed us here
seeks to take back this land with force
disguised as sympathy."

From communal weatherization
to peyote songs, regional and world
affairs, his bilingual eloquence
made topical events old news.
Every other topic a prophecy come true.

After an incident in the Badlands
(on a roadside town noted for its
commercialized springwater) when
cinder rocks had been deliberately
placed in his food — some of which
he had already ingested — he no longer
believes *trapping* is limited to his kind.
"I distrust capsules to begin with, and now
I am wary of cooks who are able to look out
at customers from their greasy kitchens.
But aspirins are my salvation. Rural
physicians refuse to prescribe codeine
and Valium on the premise *we* have no
reason to get headaches or depression."
We respond with an analogy:
if we were in Russia, the allotment
of vodka could not even begin to alleviate
our pain. Gravel is basically harmless,
but the message from the Badlands
restaurant is lucid.

Over pheasant omelettes and wine
he offers an explanation about his obsession
with technology.
"It may seem a contradiction,
but those cassette tapes on the wall
are the intellectual foundation
of my progeny."
Everyone laughs at the subliminal
connection to the earphones
and where they are placed,
breaking the tension.
We are accustomed
to his condescending attitude,
but underneath our Transformation Masks

we respect the old man, Bumblebee,
for he has retained the ability to understand
traditional precepts and myths. Moreover,
he understands the need to oppose
"outside" mining interests.

As he lights the candle on the mirrored
sconce, he translates our thoughts.
"Adjusting and manipulating
the strings and pulleys
of the exterior/interior masks
requires work at all levels.
The best test is the supernatural:
how to maintain calmness during its
manifestation; to witness and experience it
as it simply is, rather than camouflage it through
rational explanation."

In the gradual darkness our conversation
centers on Northern Lights:
celestial messengers in green atomic oxygen,
highlighted by red — the color of our impending
nuclear demise.
A hand-rolled cigarette begins
to glow from Bumblebee's lips.
Silhouetted against a white kitchen
cabinet, he rises from the sofa chair
and unfolds his transparent wings.
Just when we feel the motion of his wings
the candle goes out.

Before suggesting a drive in his pickup
to Lone Ranger to see the Helena Whiteskins
gamble in handgames with the Continental Dividers,
he reviews the strategy of the tripartite powers:
the Lynx claims Afghanistan and Poland;
the Serpent feels threatened and cannot
choose sides. Having ravaged what he
can't ravage anymore, the Eagle
becomes vulnerable. Once the Three
(volcanic) Sisters in California,

Oregon and Washington decide
to speak, the Missouri River
will reroute itself.
Satellites are taking photographs
of our sacred minerals from space,
revealing what we can't see but know
is there.
"In time we'll become prosperous,
or else we'll become martyrs
protecting the vast resources
of the Well-Off Man Mountains . . .
The force that placed us here
cannot be trusted."

THE FIRST DIMENSION
OF SKUNK

It is the middle of October
and frosted leaves
continue to introduce
their descent as season
and self-commentary.
On the ground yellow-jacket
bees burrow themselves
into the windfall apples.
On the house the empty body shells
of locusts begin to rattle with
the plastic window covering
torn loose the night previous
in the first sudden gusts of wind.
South of the highway bridge
two extinct otters are seen
by Selene's father while
setting traps.
"Mates swimming;
streamlined and playing
games along the Iowa River."
In the midst of change
all it takes in one anachronism,
one otter whistle.

For us, it began with the healthy-
looking salamander who stopped our car.
So last night we stood in the cold
moonlight waiting for the black
coyote. No animal darted
from tree to tree, encircling us.
There was a time in an orange grove
next to the San Gabriel Mountains
when I was surrounded by nervous
coyotes who were aware
of the differences
between thunder
and an earth tremor.

Selene motioned for me to stand
still, and the moonlit foothills
of Claremont disappeared.
An owl began to laugh.
I remained quiet and obliged
her gesture not to mimic its laugh,
for fear we might accidently trigger
the supernatural deity it possesses
to break this barrier —
and once again find ourselves
observing a ball of fire
rise from an abandoned garden
which separates into four fireflies
who appear like four distant jets
coming into formation
momentarily
before changing into one intense
strobe light,
pulsating inside an apple tree,
impervious to hollow-point bullets,
admissions of poverty and car lights.

We stood without response
and other disconnected thoughts came.
From the overwhelming sound
of vehicles and farm machinery,
together with the putrid odor
of a beef slaughterhouse,
such anticipation
seemed inappropriate.
Whoever constructed
the two railroad tracks
and highways through Indian land
must have planned and known
that we would be reminded daily
of what is certainty.
In my dream the metal
bridge plays an essential part
and subsequent end of what
was intended to occur.
I would speak to the heavy
glass jar, telling it

the paper bullet
was useless underwater.

Three days ago, in the teeth
of Curly and Girl, a skunk
was held firmly and shook
until lifeless.
The first evening
we hear its final death call.
At the same hour the second night
we hear it again. The third night-
sound is more brave and deliberate;
it waits to blend with the horn
of an oncoming Northwestern train,
forcing us to step backward,
taking random shots at objects
crashing through the brush.

We have a theory that Destiny
was intercepted, that the Executioner
ran elsewhere for appeasement.
We also think the skunk's
companion returned on these nights
to mourn a loved one,
but all had to be deleted,
leaving us more confused.

Yesterday, we examined the dead
skunk and were surprised to find it
three times less the size I first
saw it with Mr. D.
My parents offered an explanation.
"A parrot or a pelican on their
migratory route."
With our surroundings
at someone else's disposal,
all we have are the embers
and sparks from our woodstove
and chimney: the fragrance
to thwart the supernatural.

MESKWAKI TRIBAL CELEBRATION SONGS

Flag Song:

Ma ni ma wa wi ka	This flag
ta na se ki	shall wave
ke ki we o ni.	forever.

Akwi tta ka na kwa	No, not ever
ni ka ski te a te ki	shall it be overtaken
tta ki a na to wa ta	by men of many languages —
ma ni ke ki we o ni.	this flag.

Veteran's Song:

We ta se a ki	These veterans
wa tti na ni mi	are the reason we (are able to)
a kwi.	dance (in celebration).

Round Dance Song for Veterans:

Tte ma na	This German,
ne ma yo a	I made him cry.
wa wo si ta	His father
ma yo to ki.	must cry now as well.

WE TA SE NA KA MO NI,
VIET NAM MEMORIAL

1982

Last night when the yellow moon
of November broke through the last line
of turbulent Midwestern clouds,
a lone frog, the same one
who probably announced
the premature spring floods,
attempted to sing.
Veterans' Day, and it was
sore throat weather.
In reality the invisible musician
reminded me of my own doubt.
The knowledge that my grandfathers
were singers as well as composers —
one of whom felt the simple utterance
of a vowel made for the start
of a melody — did not produce
the necessary memory or feeling
to make a *We ta se Na ka mo ni,*
Veterans' Song.
All I could think of
was the absence of my name
on a distant black rock.
Without this monument
I felt I would not be here.
For a moment I questioned
why I had to immerse myself
in country, controversy, and guilt;
but I wanted to honor them.
Surely, the song they presently
listened to along with my grandfathers
was the ethereal kind which did not stop.

RACE OF THE KINGFISHERS: IN NUCLEAR WINTER

1.

Nobody on earth has a book of matches.
The German-silver tobacco box
and the optical burning lens
which has been built into its lid
is useless on gray blustery days.
For the moment, however, the mirrorlike
antique represents a star on the walnut
coffee table next to the iron striker,
flint and black antelope tine.
"This arrangement," notes
the elderly man named Bumblebee,
"is the tribal celestial system."
He illustrates this concept
through the quick sculpturing
of minature Sturgeon and Kingfisher
effigies in the frosted dirt.
I urge myself to pronounce
and memorize this sequence
correctly. *Should I ever see*
the real Night Sky:
The Child-Twin is trapped
between two of the brightest
stars in the Orion constellation,
and the child's earthly counterpart
is an air bubble, moving in accordance
to the pressure of our combined weight
beneath the clear river ice.

Stars have been hiding though,
and the eight snowdrift formations
cover the landscape without order.
I think of Polynesians who cannot
navigate in darkness over the ocean.
Startled by a rushing noise,
we look upward: lost seagulls

propel themselves against
the onslaught of snowflakes.

Unaffected by flood sounds
and ice jams, a lone frog —
the invisible musician — begins to emit
a low mournful song of tribute
to men-relatives whose names
are carved on a rock.
We understand
part of the song goes to men
who became an Indochina memory
after their return home.
Although they are gone,
they frequent our dreams:
two Bloody Mary drinks, a silk
navigator's scarf and golden
shoulder braids. On a concrete bridge
where giant frothy waves crash to an unseen
ocean, we honor them in the same
breath as the Trung Sisters.
This indefinite hour when
the river carries the wreath
northward — the wrong way.

2.

Above us, through the lodge portal,
the sun's double appears and causes
insects to release their numb bodies
from the ceiling into flight.
We question which myth foretold
of this neverending storm.
Through the thin wall, a voice
informs us we've lost controllable
fire. In a gesture made by thoughtless
men, we invite the voice to sit with us.
But when a child-entity enters our lodge,
wearing a perforated parka, we shield
our eyes from starlight coming through
clothes of poverty.

Each social order of the Locust
and Vulture worlds we inhabit
disagrees with our principal
belief. From each world we learn
wooden stakes cannot be twisted
to make our faces young. When
artificial intestines cease
to pulsate with the land
we will disappear again.

Motivated by tall, jagged mountains
encircled by clouds, eagles and pine
saplings, we try to make ourselves
credible to the Salamander
who was among the first
creatures.

If Paracelsus only knew . . .

3.

Outside in the wintry wind,
elegantly dressed women dance around us,
holding silver saxophones. They pretend
to smoke these instruments. Before
building up courage to step outside
and ask for a precious match
from the observers, I think
of Sherlock Holmes and his double-
brimmed hat, wondering whether
he could have solved the mystery
of the missing Night-Sky.
Upon my return, the old man
hands me a crumpled cigarette.
After a short pause for a light,
he takes a drag and talks in his smoke.
"Imported beer makes me philosophical . . ."
Later, in a demanding, raspy tone,
he asks if I have more canned beef
or Dutch beer. My wife, Selene, is offended,

but she shrugs it off. (Her eyes tell me
she knows something we don't.)

Pointing to the woman dancers,
our metamorphic guest narrates
the meaning of their intricate steps:
"In their Kingfisher costumes, they will
adjust with strings and pulleys the bird's
facial expressions while reciting complex
prose from within. Their purpose is
to apprise us of the Aurora Borealis,
and how such lights will bring
the true end." During a break
before the race of these spirits,
several dance attendants walked
up to the birds and laid out
blankets beside them, displaying
mementoes from previous Flag Wars.
"Simply by inhaling their air
with imaginary straws," whispers
our guest, "we derive good luck."

4.

Rappeling on their life strings,
caterpillars slowly stream down
from the intersecting lodge poles.
Without the presence of a healthy
cooking flame, they descend into
cool ashes. As fiery sparks begin
to materialize on an overturned skillet,
the caterpillars stop.
I resolve that wounded men
are being retrieved or dug out
somewhere in the Persian terrain.

Acknowledging the need for conflict,
and citing the story where the Heron
flew over Montana, following
the Missouri River,
familiarizing itself

with the land of Afterlife,
I rise from my chair and walk
towards the octagon drum.
Before I have a chance
to tighten the glossy drumhide
with the antelope tine,
I find myself standing in blue
tropical water. Like an infant
I try to maintain my stance,
but a huge fish swirls by,
sending a wave through
my tremulous body.

5.

Before our elderly guest left,
content that *Race of the Kingfishers*
coincided with his goal, he knelt
on the floor again and doubled
his right hand into a fist as if
he was about to send forth a marble.
Instead, he drew diagrams of the earth's
interior with lines of black sand.

As the blizzard changed into harmless clumps
of wet snow, the candlelight became steady
and bright. I thought about a painting
I had stored long ago: in dynamic
poster colors, an individual
with ironed Levis and cowboy boots
sits in a jetseat with his brown
crooked hand clutching a plastic
cocktail glass, and the window beside
him shows snowcapped mountains
with a city below them protruding
from mud. (I knew then that our
beginning was to be our end.)
I found and unwrapped the painting,
wiped the grime from the acetate cover
and read its title: *Indian Subject Asleep
On Flight 544 After Lecture On Tribal
Prophecy.*

6.

The next day when I met him
on the community's drift-covered road,
he explained his temperament was a result
of marital concerns. I said it made
no difference to my esteem, that Selene
knew all the facts. Afterwards, he showed
me his Czech cutbead buckle:
a moon of half-green and half-red beads
divided by a single horizontal line
of pearl beads. "It looks pretty good,"
I said. "A simple idea," he replied,
"but they are colors of sanctity."
I continued my walk, feeling glad
alcohol had not ruined my day.
Or his. "By the way," he said
sternly after we had walked
a few paces from each other
like chivalrous foes,
"you have a bug in your ear!"
In my heart I thought:
Why would anyone want me
under surveillance?
But my left ear had been humming.
When I turned around, three conspicuous men
with recording apparatus and earphones
tried to act as if they couldn't hear me.
In their pretense to walk into the snow-
blind, they stumbled when I spoke
to them.

NOTHING COULD TAKE AWAY THE BEAR-KING'S IMAGE

At first I thought I would feel
guilty in not missing you,
that despite its unfortunate
occurrence,
I would see you again
(exactly the way you were
before a hunter's arrow
glanced off some willows —
lodging near the pulsating song
of the Red Earth heart)
either here,
or towards that memorable direction
near the oily air of Los Angeles
where once a Zuni Indian companion
peered into a telescope aimed
at the Orion constellation:
"These three faint stars
are known for their alignment
rather than by four
of the bright stars which
frame them."

While we were sitting
on a manicured knoll
positioned above a Greek theatre,
we heard the distant skirling
sound
of Scottish bagpipes
coming through the eucalyptus trees.
We went to them, and there,
the astronomer-physicist
invited us to share his interest
in the night skies he was playing for.
He told a story of this Greek hunter
composed of stars;
the "Three-Stars-In-A-Row"
were his belt.

257

"I think that's me, grandfather,"
responded my Zuni companion,
"but I will believe you more
if you sell us your Scotch whiskey —
and consider the magnitude of my belief
if I told you the bubbles of my Creator's
saliva made the stars, grandson."
"Grandfather? Grandson? In the same
sentence? I am not related to you
in any way!" demurred the scholarly man.
The two Hispanics, Sergio & Camacho,
who were with us reaffirmed the Zuni's
request by bumping the academician
with their expanded chests.
"Grandfather, Grandson,"
they repeated.
Later, with erratic wind-notes
and chinking necklace shells,
my companion tripped and fell on
the professor's bagpipes
as he was completing
his third revolution
around the observatory.
He rolled down the sandy incline
breaking the instrument
into several pieces.
Suddenly, the professor's eyes
possessed a wild gleam,
a distant fire we hadn't seen before;
a nebula of sorts.
He knelt next to the dead instrument
and began to weep.
"My dear chanter! My drone!"
Like gentlemen, Sergio & Camacho
offered to pay for the irreplaceable
antique parts, but it was too late.
We left (no, we fled from)
the observatory.

Back at the Greek theatre,
we found solace by the singing
of round and grass dance songs

with three Caucasians:
one jeweler, one ROTC student
and one KSPC disc jockey,
until we were greeted
by Sioux voices from the dark.
There was immediate silence,
and then the Sioux National Anthem:
"The United States flag will stand forever.
As long as it stands the people will live
and grow; therefore, I am doing this
say the Indian soldier boys."
The radio announcer advised us
the voice was amplified,
possibly by a handheld system.
Pretty soon, we were surrounded
by figures wearing bronze helmets.
The jeweler whispered to us.
"They look like Mudheads with metallic paint."
The military student observed and commented
on their evenly-spaced formation.
Several descended the stone steps
and their boot heels echoed
onto the stage.
When they got close
with their glistening visors,
nightsticks and badges,
we were bewildered.
The police officer explained
that he was a boy scout leader
and learning Siouan was essential.
"Would you boys consider singing
for our troop in Pomona?"
he queried before stating
the purpose of his visit.
"What disturbance?" we asked
in regard to bagpipes and walked back
to our individual dormitory rooms.
We called each other on the phone,
laughing at times, exchanging crazy
warhoops in a warm California night;
that ancient but comical time and place
where we hypothesized the draft

which lifted Marilyn Monroe's dress
came from the San Andreas Fault.
When it shifted, Orozco's murals
in Frary Hall actually moved,
responding to the land wave
and the force of the Pacific Ocean.

We are endless like the Central Plains
breeze in winter which makes the brittle
oak leaves whisper in unison of this
ethereal confidence.
Nothing could take away
the Bear-King's own image
who is human and walks.
There remains a bottle of champagne
beside the charred concrete block;
the half-smoked cigarette
of cornhusk and Prince Albert tobacco
which was propped next
to the green bottle
has disappeared
in the snowdrift.

The Spearbow Priest hasn't been summoned.
In the tribal gymnasium, exercise
equipment is marked by the greasy
handprints of a phantom infant.
The caretaker's two bows
and their arrows lie unpropelled.
The crooked snakelike arm doesn't
have the strength to draw back
the taut string, which would
have triggered an old-time
message to the brain.
On top of a moonlit hill
stands a boy whose lithe body
has been painted black
with numerous light-blue spots.
He signals us to follow him,
and he lights small fires
along the way.

Inside the earth-mound,
a small man in a bright-red headband
places an arrow in the bowstring
of his left hand which is bent
like a bow.
He explains the meaning
of the arrow's crest.
"From the birds the bison dreams about.
This shaft of wood tipped with sharpened flint,
together with the wolfskin draped over the hunter
crouching low against the salty earth . . ."

NINETEEN EIGHTY THREE

1.

It is January —
and simply because
the rain failed to change
into snow
the quiet river
has risen to flood stage.
Half-frozen rainwater
fills into a nearby pond
where once the sound
of frogs, crickets,
mosquitoes and birds
permeated the humid
summer night:
narcosis through
the sound of an open
window. Tomorrow
young children will
pretend to skate
over the thick pond ice,
but each day their figures
will slowly descend
into the ground,
reminding us
of mythical Rolling
Heads playing hockey.
The rainwater will evaporate
and ice will succumb
to the daily game.
Winter's indecision
makes us feel safe.
An elder, however,
would say "You're
basically unprepared."
No matter how *balanced*
one's mentality,
one's physicality.

2.

The gentle appearance
of the Female Death Light
from Wisconsin
takes place
in the center
of a soybean field.
Two times, a slow fire.
Inside the hollow wall
a mouse takes a chance
during our rumination
to weep like a human.
Throughout the neighborhood
the four-legged sentinels,
especially the all-white ones,
signal each other of this
Incongruity: a shadow
of an unknown tall being
stands in the flash
of lightning.

COOL PLACES OF TRANSFORMATION

Due to the flood-level force
of the Wapsipinicon River
each grain of sand
which has been loosened
from the radiant bone-white
beach, tumbles and disappears
into the swift, opaque undercurrent.
Slowly, in my desire for sleep,
I envision myself as this crescent-
shaped beach, alive but pensive,
feeling acquiescence as my senses
are gradually being divided,
examined, and swept away
by images of abandon and dream:

One of my ears detaches itself
from me and bounces along the river
floor and chooses wisely to ignore
pleas from the delicate sense
of *thought* lodged in the tan rocks
of a catfish sanctuary.
Both of my hands are able
to stop themselves in spite
of their inability to discern
exactly where assistance is needed.
Emulating the badger, my nose
burrows into the silt for no
reason. Although one of my eyes
knows from experience that long,
ominous shadows represent cool places
of transformation, its brother-eye
chooses to enter a desolate checker-
board alley (like the kind in a De
Chirico painting) and extricate
the deity who sacrificed its once
eagle beauty to shape earth's landscape.

Suddenly, after clouds of mud

and silt have been replaced
by the aroma of spearmint,
the senses form themselves
into a vulture who surveys
the mountains and glaciers
of Greenland, reliving their
painful Creation.

Moments later, I awaken
to the faint sounds of a mosquito
in ascent, escaping after it has drawn
metal-tasting blood from my chest
with a horn. On the mule deer hide
of an octagon drum, I see four
killer whales suspended
in the watery sunlight.
I feel loss in being neither
winged or aquatic creature.
Somewhere in the sky's glare,
mosquitoes will gather in clans
for a feast, and someone will rationalize
a greater entity could have done worse,
"such as the bluejay," wounding me
without ceremony . . .

THREE VIEWS OF A NORTHERN PIKE

With a small round mirror
submerged upright
in an olive-green basin
of cool pumpwater,
I am hoping through
subtle maneuver
of this "true picture"
that the young Northern Pike,
held captive, will see
its majestic self
and therefore adduce
that the stagnant pool
(where I seined it)
would have evaporated
or become congested
with autumn leaves,
anyway.

During night or dawn,
in a flight of acceptance,
this fish will consider
the ebony cricket.
If it should eat something,
a leg or antenna,
or acknowledge itself,
my presence,
through fin flutter,
the thought of a four foot
forty-five pound predator
encircling us
in an aquarium
built between
the library shelves
will transform to love
and commitment.

Stationary, the pike hovers
before its prehistoric reflection;

its feathery rainbow-fringed gills
pulsating more evenly.
Soon, a large spot similar
to a Union Jack flag
appears underneath its lucid skin:
I see the fish as a British Harrier jet.

As I take notes and sketch
the various perspectives
of clupeiforme, Woodland Indian
and convex mirror,
my eyes cannot shake
the transparent effect of water.
For a moment, I believe
it is a sanctimonious sign,
warning me.

Later, my respect is overruled
by an old time cerebral message:
should the fish be inverted
in the morning,
struggling to hold
its life,
I cannot keep it;
should it die before
reaching the river rapids,
I must use it as a lure.

DEBUT OF THE WOODLAND DRUM

At the place
where Midwestern glaciers
supposedly came to a stop,
having created the last
buttes and stone cliffs
along the Mississippi
(which would one day remind
extraterrestials of home planet
and thus establish a colony
in the name of Scandanavia),
we listened to Debra Harry
of Blondie sing ATOMIC
four hours from Oneida,
Wisconsin.

A WOMAN'S NAME IS IN THE SECOND VERSE: EARTHQUAKES AND PARALLELS

In the dream before I noticed the predawn thunder
was actually an earth tremor, Lillian Nicotine
of Pinelodge Lake, resplendent in her purple
silk blouse and skirt, came up to me
and whispered unfamiliar pedagogical terms
in a Canadian dialect. (I knew it was half
in reference to a question made sixteen years
previous at the "54th Parallel" conference
on Algonquin linguistics.) Overtaken by memory
of her beauty, it took a few moments before
I fully understood what she was saying.
"Did you hear that?" she asked in alarm
as lightning began to flash through low clouds.
"The static in His PA system is merely thunder —
a signal that a song more powerful than the hymn
of angels is forthcoming."

When the thunder stopped, a song in supernatural
wattage began. It came down in falsetto,
reciting words of beauty, of totality,
of purpose. *"Ni ke ta ke be na,
ni ke ta ke be na na ka mo ni. Wa ba to tti
me to se ne ni a e na a ka wa ni!*
We will throw it out, we will throw out
this song. Show the people your dancing ability!"
Although I believed the source was sacred,
I recognized the voice of Maker belonged
to Alfred Potato, a mortal. (It almost occurred
to me then that the last time I saw Lillian,
a Middle Eastern lover had been too liberal
with his fists on her body, that I had even paid
her a visit: a fool with new flowers in hand,
lamenting her bruised body at the PHS Hospital
on St. Michael's Road. But the thought dissipated.)
The Maker's voice is like any human voice,
I said to myself. Like Alfred's. Twice my eyes

clouded. Hector and Sam Reveres Nothing —
victims of Indochina after the fact.
They were the only ones who could dance
for Earth.

Lillian placed her cool palm over my mouth
and said I should not inquire, offer explanations
or formulate a theory about the clear, wavering
voice that travelled over the landscape. I looked
at her beautifully slanted eyes in the lightning.
The infant-like skin on her nose was almost
transparent. She held on to my arm
and intentionally brushed her soft breasts
against my elbow. Her faint perfume intensified
my brain-induced paralysis.

After we walked in the opposite direction
of the cloudburst, we entered a green valley
lit by the summer sun. Squinting, we looked
at each other to reaffirm our pact, but we
had to turn around, pause, and marvel
at the point where the wall of dark rain
divided the region in two like a security light
defining ownership in a quiet rural evening.

To the north, a stone hill with terraces
delivered springwater into a small pond
filled with young walleye and pike fish
whose shiny gills pulsated in contentment
over the volcanic sand. To the south,
a row of apple trees stood under the fervent
attention of yellow jacket bees. When the first
minor tremor loosened and sent clumps of creosote
down the stovepipe, I saw Cody, the coyote-dog,
alive again, chasing grasshoppers and kicking
rocks over a dirt road. Next, thinking
I was in the path of mortar shell-fire,
I had to cringe under a star blanket
when the second landwave banged the stovepipe
inside the brick chimney. The third quake
shattered glass in the frames of doors

and windows. But the fourth — the fourth
broke the earth open.

The dormitory building I slept in named Smiley
toppled over the white Porsche that would have taken
me to LAX. *Plum blossom witchcraft,* I thought
the moment I heard listening devices coming down
through the twisted water pipes and tennis court
concrete. I woke up and realized the "Throw Out Song"
was the Maker's own summation of life that should
have been. Through the dark, inverted mass
a voice spoke out: "Is anybody down there?
If you are, call out and we will try to locate you.
Any sound you are able to make will help us."
There was a click and then silence.
I wanted to respond terribly, but the thick
bloodclot in my nose and mouth, along with intense
chest pain prevented it.

From somewhere below where I was suspended
a cry came out. "Oh God, please help me!"
It was the Caucasian who lived across the hall;
I recognized his slightly effeminate voice
from the rappeling practice he did with club
members from floor to floor in Smiley.
Although part of the cast iron railing,
which once held the mountain climbers' ropes
and clamps, was now embedded in my chest,
my heart continued to work. As the weight
of the earth shifted above me, I could feel
the stairway railings grind into the plaster
behind me. I saw myself as a spear-impaled fish
unable to move as the wooden pole and barbed tines
pushed me deeper into the silt and mud
for good measure.

MESKWAKI LOVE SONG

Ne kwi na ta we na be na so
a ka me e ki
e ki wi ne o na ni.

Ka na i skwe wa ba mo ni
ke wa wa - wa wa sa se na ma wi no
ke wi a wa ni.

I would like to be taken (romantically)
in the distant forest
where I have been seeing you.

At least with your mirror
reflect, reflect for me
where you are.

GREEN THREATENING CLOUDS

"Paint these green threatening clouds
a rose color," said Elvia near my shoulder.
"I mean around the fluffy sides to at least
give credence to these ceramic-looking pitchers
and their red corrugated brims. And how will you
convey the phenomena of luminous mountain plants
when they're nocturnal?"
She had two good points as far
as biology and the dispersal of colors
was concerned, but I was debating where
to hang the pitchers whose poisonous
contents, if consumed, would make this
jungle a lovely place to close one's eyes
in permanence and see that far-ahead time
when gravity-wise hawks would splinter
my hip bone against a mountainside
repeatedly for marrow access,
a time in respect when young bull
elks would nudge their antlers against
my half-submerged and decayed antlers
in the tundra, a time when my arctic
shadow would claim pieces of ice
as descendants and incubate them,
arguing with any penguin over
their ownership . . .

Outside, a Midwestern cardinal hovered
under the roof of my parent's prayer lodge
and delicately maneuvered itself to the tip
of an icicle for a nonexistent drop of water.
In the snow-covered garden, a bluejay
disappeared into a brittle corn husk
and gave it momentary life, but none
was received from a dance made from
hunger. (Here we cannot migrate
to low altitude for tropical weather
and abundant food. Instead, like cultures
who wait for their savior, we wait for
a young man who has a neverending source

273

of food in his Magic Tablecloth.)
In our efforts to help the hungry birds,
we impale a slice of bread on a treelimb,
but it freezes and becomes a violent wind
sculpture. At thirteen below zero, a poorly
clothed child walks by with a lonely sled
in hand.

And then Elvia began talking about Saskatchewan.
"I dreamt of a large green eagle, and it was
speaking to me in French. I understood that
the eagle was an elder, who had flown *down*
in response to a song when a person is allowed
to leave its body."
"Does such a song exist?" I questioned.
"Of course," she replied. "Green. Such an
important color."

MY GRANDMOTHER'S WORDS (AND MINE) ON THE LAST SPRING BLIZZARD

The snow has fallen in variations.
Each variation has a meaning
which goes back to our *Creation*.
This morning, for instance,
branches broke under
the wet snow's weight.

Last night, in the snowstorm,
anyone could've gotten lost.

Such was the time before
our moment when the Good
eluded Evil . . .

(Despite a winter of doubt,
I owe my existence to the ally
who now rests on the ground outside
with *His* brilliant white blanket
covering the green grass-shoots
of another year.)

IF THE WORD FOR WHALE IS RIGHT

The old tribal messenger
whose grass-legbands
glided silently over
the sparse woodland
and prairie
began to sense
snowflakes landing
on his face.
He momentarily broke
from his stride,
but resumed it after
the realization that snow
was an ally:
a testimonial
opposite from
the fog.

Inspired by his commitment
to keep following
an invisible trail,
impervious to weather
and obstacle,
he wanted to compose
a song for his mentor
No no ke, Hummingbird,
whose rapid wings
fanned rocks, thorns
and branches aside
in front of him.

When the cold waters
of the Mississippi River
came up to his neck,
he listened to
the frenetic drumming
of his heart and lungs,
and then determined how
the song should go,
combining tune, lyric,

breath and situation
together.

"This very moment and ever since
my investiture as a divine runner,
I think of your help."

As he attempted to swim around
dangerous blocks of drifting ice,
he noticed the dark fins of *Me tti na me*
parallel to him,
silhouetted against a sandy beach.
Right away he thought:
A song for him, too!

Of course, a century later
his idyllic grandchildren
(while listening to their elders
sing inside the geodesic
dome-shaped lodge)
would fail to associate
or understand
the archaic term
for the nonexistent
whale.

THREE TRANSLATED POEMS FOR OCTOBER

Old woman, I hope that at least
you will watch me in the future
when I am an elderly man —
so my baggy clothes
do not catch fire
when I socialize
with the young people
as they stand around
the campfire intoxicated.
Of course, I will tell them
worldly things.

    / / /

Now that the autumn season
has started, one suddenly
realizes the act of living
goes fast.
Sometimes the spring
is that way too:
the green so quick.
Thirty-two years of age I am.
Box elder leaves are being shaken
by the cold rain and wind.
In the tree's nakedness
there stands a man,
visible.

    / / /

Although there is yet
a lot of things to do,
surprisingly, I have this urge
to go fishing.
They say the whites
in town will pay
one hundred dollars

to whoever catches
the largest channel catfish
or flathead.
You know I like to fish.
We could invite and feed
lots of friends.
Plus, purchase
a cast iron woodstove
since the business committee
has ignored our weatherization
application, but Bingo
is on the agenda.

JOURNAL ENTRY, NOVEMBER 12, 1960

Fred Bloodclot Red's Song to be Used
in the Spring for the Long, Narrow Fish
Who is Also an Eagle:

"I hide the two suns
from striking my face,
but I feel their warmth
equally on my palm.

They are brothers:
one born from water (and
related to the trapped
bubble under the ice),
the other sky . . .

In the shadow
made from my hand,
I feel their warmth
equally."

THE BLACK ANTELOPE TINE

When Lucretia Rude Youth took out her childhood
mementoes from the sewing box and placed them
carefully over the table, the kitchen air,
although imperceptible at first, became cooler
than the high waters that drove us to her house
for shelter. To perhaps conceal this change,
venison and coffee had been prepared —
our arrival anticipated.

The meal's warmth made me think of turtles
basking on peeled logs over the tribal dam.
That was the last day I was comfortable
before rains filled the lowlands.
We were going to stay, explained
the victims in us . . . But any plan
of escape, interjected Cree, is acceptance
of danger by morning. Which was true.
The flood history of the Swan Root
was depicted on her face. As a girl,
she said, I dove for *e si wa wa na ni,*
clam eggs or pearls. We listened, but
something was amiss.

Was it the night? Or was it the finely-
clothed figurines whose plaid material
resembled shirts we used to wear?
Did our frightened eyes reflect like
marble stars in the searchlights
of supernatural hunters?

Jesus, I once dreamt of doll-sized
human beings — six intoxicated dwarfs
who asked to be rolled together in a towel.
Put us in a trash can, they pleaded,
before we get arrested. They eventually
suffocated because I forgot to pick them up.
And now, here they were in the form of antique
toys. An alcohol-related tragedy.

Cree tried to keep our attention on Philippine
coins, old wax seals and war photographs,
but I was soon conscious of another strength —
cool and invisible — emanating from a cast iron
toy kettle. Her narrations about the deformed
pearl hunter became inaudible as autumn rain
exploded on the roof, sending slivers of light
out into the yard. Sleet. *There was this kind
of power once: tribal celebration dancers
flashed their sequins under the nightlights
and the ground bloated beneath their feet
until we all stood on what seemed a little
earth. We attempted to balance on its
curvature. Yet the dancers danced when
regalias alone could have disabled anyone.
Sharp triangles of bone in the heel and instep.
Roots to combat sorcery.*

Every article in Cree's kitchen,
including the woodstove and Selene's face,
was concentric. A slice of French bread
levitated over my palm. Beside two figurines
from the morning of forgotten dwarfs,
the odious mass of a Spanish galleon
broke through the toy kettle and hovered
under the ceiling. It was the same ship
whose ochre clouds held me down as a child
near death.

I found myself in the arms of my elderly father.
He was taking me to Well-Off Man's gathering
where I would soon be spoon-fed with *amanita* tea
to subdue my seizures. I knew all of this
and I wanted to say so. When we entered
the canvas and tin-covered lodge,
Calvin Star, the appointed drum-maker,
was winding a thin rope around the tripod
legs of an overturned kettle. In his delicate
but rapid hands, the black antelope tine
which would be used to tighten and tune
the drum sparkled in the kerosene lamp's
bronze light.

QUAIL AND HIS ROLE IN AGRICULTURE

"Now it's here
that time which
was once forthcoming
for us to remember
our older/younger brother
Quail," was how I composed
a song for John Louis.
Though I had very little
to do with him socially
or the family way,
ever since my cousin
acknowledged his unrequited
love fifteen years ago,
I thought it befitting
to present this song
to him before the next
memorial.

As I began to drum on the car's
dashboard with my fingers,
several horticulturalists
who were waiting their turn
at the Tastee Freez line
looked my way. Their clothes
were resplendent: bright baseball
caps with fertilizer logos,
ironed overalls, and new workshirts;
but their faces were tired and expression-
less. With the constant drone of harvesting
machinery in their ears, they probably
thought the tapping was yet another
mechanical trouble to contend with,
for they were the only ones to turn
their heads. The rest just wanted
to order.

It was a hot September day, and we
had all stopped to have strawberry

sundaes: I, to celebrate my song;
and they, to soothe the grain and dust
in their throats. Midwesterners, all,
standing in the monolithic shadow
of a hydraulic platform, which lifted
the semi-truck's cab to the sky
to violently shake and dislodge
its cargo of yellow corn —
the historic sustenance
which was now to some
a symbol of abject poverty.
For others, like myself and all
my grandfathers before me, it continues
to be a transmitter of prayer.
Beautiful yellow corn . . .

COLLEEN'S FAITH

Colleen sweeps the floor
carefully and rearranges
the furniture as if guests
were expected. The crooked
branch, however, which measures
the river's depth in the yard
is an unerring reminder that
the earth's cool and dank
breeze is intended for us
alone. Every time we begin
to forget this ominous fact,
a strong, deliberate current
shakes and momentarily drowns
a row of berry bushes. For
the sixth night, the reflection
of our houselights will shimmer
against the land's distant
circumference. With the community's
great "registered" cottonwood
smoldering under an overcast sky,
no one will believe we are here
in the middle and deepest part
of the flood. On the sandy rapids
over the gravel road, old men
who have kept a day-long vigil
for black, ribbon-like forms
of leeches have gone home
to count their bait earnings,
leaving behind them the incessant
laughs of children who contradict
our plight as they swim like
strong carp over the hidden
culvert's upsurge of brown
water.

FRED BLOODCLOT RED'S COMPOSITION: FOR USE ON THE THIRD NIGHT OF FOOTSTEPS

The lower protruding jaw
of the Eagle-Fish is translucent.
This nightmare is the first thing
we see swimming warily around
the moss-covered stone bend
of a deep, clear river.

We cannot remain as silent
as the Blessing Constellations;
in haste, I instruct you to say
to yourself for Him: Father,
for the reason you are part-
water, part-sky, I am still
the trapped bubble under
the ice.

And still, I have not abused
anyone vocally or physically,
nor have I thought ill-will
to relative and friend. That
I will confess to anyone . . .

The cigarette you smoke,
which lingers in the oak
treetops above my room,
is the same brand as mine.

ALWAYS IS HE CRITICIZED

There was this dance procession
I was a part of, and we were all males
following one another, demonstrating
our place in Black Eagle Child society
with flexed chest muscles and clenched fists.
(I later thought this image a cultural
paradox when some of us were supported
on income made by women. We were still
warlike but perennially unemployed.)
We were singing an energetic, non-
religious song, but we gave it
reverence as if it were one,
admonishing anyone who forgot
such compositions could not
have been made by humans.
The leader started the loud
repetitive verse and we quickly
joined in with voices amplified
by mountainous terrain. "Always
is he criticized, always is he
criticized — in the manner of a pig
I dance."

On our blistered hands and knees
we crawled up the difficult mountainside.
Sometimes we depended on the heart's blissful
intonation for dreams when powdery
snow incapacitated our bodies.
As the blizzard left for earth,
we saw the still, inflated corpses
of those who succumbed to His domain.
At one point, perhaps in a moment
of fatigue, I looked down the valley
and was amazed how far we had climbed,
singing the same song.

By nightfall I was still struggling
to keep up with the dance, and several

layers of ice and snow clung to my
chilled face like an Albino Mask.
Suddenly, up ahead past the Torn
Blanket faction, the leader said something
in reference to the one flashlight we had
and the loud breathing nearby. A dim beam
was directed to a large, lumbering shadow.
And here, whether it was part of the dance
or actual fear, we cringed at the sight
of our cousin who was outfitted in a loose,
oversized bear suit. He snarled and moved
about in anger. What he didn't realize
was that a real grizzly bear was standing
beside him, foaming at the mouth. Our cousin
couldn't hear, see or feel the giant bear's
presence. But he did wince in pain as the bear
drove an arrow into his ribs. Fred Bloodclot Red
was suspended on the wooden suit support like
a crucifix.

In half-delirium and half-sleep
I thought I heard new cowboy boots
being test-walked over the thin
floor boards of our trailer.
"For New England," Fred had joked
before his demise. As a lifetime
resident of Carson Red Hat Reserve
whose sole highlight would have been
this one lecture on tribal prophecy
at Cambridge, he was embarrassed
for being dependent on his grandmother
for footwear. But he confided in us,
especially the autumn before the plane crash.

*"Ki a tti mo e ni a kwi me nwe ne
ta ma ni e na ta wi ki e ska wa ni.*
I will tell you that I do not like
your intention to travel," his grandmother
had forewarned. *"Ne ta tti na we e kwi me ko.*
It bothers me greatly." She had explained
to Fred how she sensed misfortune

through the decomposition of a potato,
how it lingered in the house for days,
that she would not find its source
until the malediction was complete.
In half-delirium and half-sleep I know
of no way to reverse Fred's impermanence.
Certain bones affixed to my limbs
will not transport me to bring him
back. An attempt at The Contrary
would only interfere with a shadow
that continually relives
its preparation for death.

THE HANDCUFF SYMBOL

We were struggling over a small pearl-
handled Saturday Night Special.
Like three angry adolescents,
so many thousands of miles
from Black Eagle Child,
we were turning an afternoon
college kegger at the Greek Theatre
into a perilous scene:

Weasel Heart, the one who held
the pistol either wanted to shoot
himself or another. A random execution
of someone, nonetheless. We pleaded
first in our language, hoping
such words and their common
sense inflections would subdue
despondency and remind him
of the acquiescent but *living*
grandfathers we represented.
"Ba ki se na no tta kwi ba
e ye ba i ko ye be te na wa tti.
Let go of the pistol before you
accidently shoot a bystander."

Like that famous war photograph
of American soldiers raising a flag
over Iwo Jima, we raised the pistol
together and waved it high above
the silhouettes of palm trees —
and it began firing. In the concrete
earth basin, sparks from the hollowpoint
shells flew out from the thin space
between cylinder and barrel.
The red muzzle flash lit
the poverty and mold
of our skeletons.

        /   /   /

Before the loudspeaker spoke,
the helicopter's spotlight
came through the windows of the log
cabin I was born in. The same greasy
curtains were there, still held
by a stone-smooth yarn string.
Over the woodstove, still unchanged
except for her dilated, opaque pupils,
Sister Theresa was sprinkling commodity
surplus flour into a skillet of watered-
down pork and beans. She was mouthing
the Spectre's command: "Surrender
yourself to piety." She then
pointed to the dried blood
I had slept on and said,
"Ke ta be kwe tti mo ne ma.
Your pillow." As I gently
touched my face for wounds,
I found a marble floating
under the skin of my right wrist.
That's when a tribal committee
member, who was acting as liaison
on behalf of the authorities,
knocked on the partially-open door.
I could see the shadow of his fat body
breathing nervously on the bright floor.
"The family of the injured party
is out there also. So there's
witnesses."

  /   /   /

I couldn't remember a damn thing
except the final humiliating moment
in being where we were, what we were about
to do. There's nothing more disgraceful
than Indians in serious trouble —
in faraway places. How we are able
to travel and meet has to be nomadic
instinct. Truth aside, we often react
like beached whales, and this culture

keeps throwing us back into the black,
chaotic sea. Although we thrash about
for our lives, however demented and painful
it has been, we drown others in the process.

         /   /   /

I am simply relating this dream
as preface to my belief they often
reoccur in reality. Sometimes in reverse.
The handcuffs, for instance, were positive.
Yet I can imagine the power of a crying
family — relatives of whoever we shot.
Point is, the next night after this dream,
a police officer actually wrapped
my bleeding palms and wrist with gauze,
and he radioed an ambulance for me.
And the gunshots? They turned out
to be my palms busting through
the hot windows of a burning
but empty house. Small caliber
gunfire can sound like glass
being broken. And the marble
under my wrist was in actuality
a hematoma or blood clotting.
But the drunk who I thought
was in the burning house asked me
for no apparent reason if I still
possessed the pistol. Instead
of being stunned by yet another
correlation, I lied and purposely
implanted a continuing vision
of this evil piece in his mind.
I could have bled to death
were it not for the gauze cuffs.

THE DREAM OF PURPLE BIRDS IN MARSHALL, WASHINGTON

My people back home love purple —
on clothes for ceremonial or everyday wear.
But the two birds who reside near the city
of Spokane, like us, wear this color as well.
On morning two, they flutter and tap
their purple bodies against our window.
They attempt to tell us something.
Or as I dread, as I have felt
through sleeplessness,
they are the once-life of two women
whose body parts lie scattered
and hidden safely under the dirt and rocks
of a railroad track —
the same one that winds through
this community, this pinetree-lined
valley. In desperation I ask one bird,
"Ka tti ya bi ke te tta wi?
What's the matter with you?"
With its purple mask and cape, the bird
hopped on a branch and turned more towards
my way as further testament:
the underside of its body was white-colored
with red speckled lines flowing from its neck
to its chest. These innocent ladies are here
somewhere, they tell me, beckoning you
from dream, from Iowa, from yourself.
Tonight, to keep all this away from me,
I will apply a thin, transparent coat
of yellow paint over the top half
of my round face: *I refuse to be*
their spiritual conduit and release
in a valley where the sun darkens early,
in a valley where a large, red fluorescent
cross is physically so much stronger
than I . . .

TWO POEMS FOR SOUTHEASTERN WASHINGTON

Steptoe Butte reigns in the moonlit clouds
over Palouse country. And they call this structure
a butte? Back home, if this rose up from the flat
farmlands it would be deemed a *Mountain that was God.*
High above is Bullchild's celestial pursuer:
Moonwoman rests her body and leg
on a communication tower.
The supernatural history
of Stars.

/ / /

Eight-wheeled tractors — not the ones
we are accustomed to seeing in Iowa —
roll over the steepest hills
with precision without the slightest
threat of tipping over. Even if they
were upside-down they would not falter
because of their even proportion
over the undulating earth. (Think
of all the farmer's lives that could
be saved by these gravity-wise machines.)
Though I have nothing to do with agriculture,
I am astounded. More so, when the giant tractors
dive, reappear and dive earthward
over the landscape, swimming
like muskrats with serious intent.

FOX GUIDES FROM LA CROSSE ON

She summoned
Fox-allies in her sleep,
and they surfaced
from roadsides and cliffs —
unafraid and concerned —
to take turns
running in front
of the Toyota
before jumping back
on the assurance
she was taken
care of.

Upon her waking
at the gas station
in Decorah, we apprised her
of the multiple appearances
on the detour where we got lost,
how in the moon's new place
they acted like guides.

Unimpressed by our story,
she said, *"A kwi ye to ki*
ta kwa o ne kwe. Hide *ta ta ki;*
ne tti ya ki te me kwe.
Why did you not run them over.
For the hide; perhaps it's expensive."

Trying once more to emphasize
their importance, we say:
"A kwi ma ma ni a bi tti ta so wi
Ne o tti ni wa ko tte a ki all year.
Not this many Fox are seen all year."

But it was no use.
She knew we never picked up
animal carcasses on trips.
It just wasn't our way,

especially to first sight
then kill. Our reverence
for her guides
was made unimportant.

"For a purpose," we later
postulated. There is no obvious
explanation to snowdrifts which
avoid the bird-shaped plants
that communicate with her.
Human-sounding voices in
their exhale of green breath . . .

SHADOWS OF CLOUDS

For Sara Jumping Eagle

From the frosted morning window I look out
at the new yard and make the mistake of thinking
a mound of gray ashes as last traces of winter
in spring. Visually, I believe bark and soot
have melted into the snow.

And then I recall all the brush that was burned
for a week to clear this "allotted tribal acre."

Why must I conjure this tortuous illusion?

When blizzards materialize from His Breath:
half a world, half a world away,
sending stars over the warm
mountain haze. Shadows of clouds
over other clouds.

MESKWAKI LOVE SONG

Ke te na,	It is true,
ke te na wa na,	It is true then,
ne ki wa tti	I am a lonely
me to se ne ni	human being.
Ke te na,	It is true,
ke te na wa na,	It is true then,
ne ki wa tti	I am a lonely
me to se ne ni	human being.
Me sko ta ka a i ki	Unfortunately, too,
ma a ki to to si wa ki	these crickets (and their singing)
ne ka ki wa tti me ko ki	make me lonely.
Ke te na,	It is true,
ke te na wa na,	It is true then,
ne ki wa tti	I am a lonely
me to se ne ni	human being.

NOTES TO THE INVISIBLE MUSICIAN

The Significance of a Water Animal — The Meskwaki word, *O ki ma,* can be translated into English as The Sacred Chief. According to my grandmother, Ada K. Old Bear, before we — the Meskwaki or Red Earth People — were sculpted from the earth, there was *O ki ma:* a human being who came from the very flesh and blood of Creator's heart; a divine decision-maker whose sole purpose in life was and is to guide us through the expanse created. My grandmother's sons, Charles and David Old Bear, are the traditional Chiefs of the Meskwaki Tribe. In 1856, their great-grandfather, *Ma mi nwa ni ke,* initiated the historic purchase and establishment of our tribal homeland in Central Iowa. Akin to the ethereal history of the *O ki ma,* the Water Animal, Muskrat or "Earth-diver" is an integral part of earth's beginnings.

The Language of Weather — It is said that whirlwinds whether comprised of dust, leaves or snow represent the eternally trapped shadows or "souls" of the deceased who have yet to be transferred ceremonially to the Hereafter and replaced by another (living person) via the Adoption Ceremony. If this ceremony isn't performed, the forgotten shadow turns into a whirlwind — or even a nocturnal bird of prey.

The King Cobra as Political Assassin — Shortly before the attempted Presidential assassination in 1981, I had a graphic dream about fighting serpents. For creative purposes I associated the serpents to the would-be assassin and the holder of the highest office in this country. As information gradually surfaced about the alleged influences of the movie "Taxi Driver" upon these events, I imagined being prescient. In the end, however, my dream was far from Hollywood's portrayal of a demented cabbie, sleazy city life and politics. The truth was, I was captivated by a strip of wilderness outside of the Settlement's borders where eagles actually stopped to rest and hunt. I once contemplated its acquisition.

The First Dimension of Skunk — One part of this poem is taken from a story entitled "The Supernatural Strobelight" (*Black Eagle Child,* University of Iowa Press). While one isn't usually required to state what is true or not, I am compelled by memory — and perhaps respect — to acknowledge the three owls, who, on one autumn night in 1980, collectively or individually, manifested themselves as a series of bizarre, transforming lights. Grace Mad Soldier and Alfred Pretty Boy-in-the-Woods offered the following possibilities on what the lights could have been: 1.) apprentices of sorcery who sought to drive us away from the isolated river bottom; 2.) ghosts from an old village which was located near our residence; 3.) the shadows or "souls" of the deceased who have not been accorded the Adoption Ceremony; 4.) a malignant, floating disease in search of a human host. For the miraculous display of flying lights we will always remember, including their mass exodus several nights later, we thought the fifth possibility was extraterrestrials. In such manifestations, however, inexplicability is a perfect mask.

Eagle Crossing, July 1975 — Composed largely from fiction but influenced in part by fragmented readings on the Blackfeet, this work is one of the eleven poems in this collection based on experimentation. Linguistically, the Meskwaki translation of the English name "Big Foot" is *Me ma ki ka ta ta* or Big Footed One, which is remarkably identical to the Blackfeet pronunciation and definition of the same name. Source: Mr. Floyd Rider, Two Medicine Lake Singers, East Glacier Park, Montana.

All Star's Thanksgiving — In November of 1965, I attended a dusk to dawn gathering where *amanita* — a mushroom with hallucinogenic properties — was ingested for religious purposes. Sensing my interest, my grandmother who was the congregation's cook at the time, encouraged further attendance. I made three visits in all before spiritual curiosity exhausted my immature mind. The songs and prayers which addressed alcoholism, extreme poverty and social repression were too vivid. To see this in my youth made me realize what the tribe had to contend with. I respected the Well-Off Man Congregation's ways but chose not to go back. To my grandmother, this was one part of the four religions in her life. She possesses an extraordinary gift for understanding other people's beliefs. But the foundation for all this is the Principal Meskwaki Belief.

The Dream of Purple Birds in Marshall, Washington — In the spring of 1987, upon our arrival at Eastern Washington University near Spokane to begin a teaching residency, Stella and I were driven by our hosts to a small community where we were to stay. As we began to descend into this picturesque valley, there was a ceaseless, disturbing feeling I had somehow visited the area before. I experienced a déjà vu of sorts, but this particular one stayed until I realized through dream or reincarnation that I had once witnessed the brutal homicide of two white women by two white men.

For several days, we were also puzzled by two birds who came to the kitchen window every morning to hover and peck at what must have been

300

their reflections. Out of this situation, including the insomnia caused by a dormitory cot, I concluded hypothetically that the birds were the "souls" of the two white women who I truly felt were buried *somewhere* along the railroad tracks south of Marshall. If they were indeed "around" I felt their salvation depended not on me but on the forty-foot high cross whose neon tubes of red towered over the quiet, unsuspecting community every night.

/ / /

Perhaps as an offshoot of how Meskwaki people traditionally viewed their dreams, this collection includes seven other poems — pages 239, 251, 269, 281, 286, 287, and 290 — that are dream-affiliated. Today the sense of mystery and respect that were once generated by this extrasensory element has diminished. But for some people, especially those who remain true to their beliefs, these glimpses from the past and future reveal what we normally wouldn't know, couldn't know.

It should be noted that in the course of all things literary, a reference to a dream in this book can be a single sentence — the "fuel" that Charles Bukowski speaks of — or it may well be the entire sequence of the dream itself. And sometimes parts from two or three dreams are combined.

/ / /

Once, somewhere far away, a graduate student asked a distinguished visiting writer what value dreams were to creative writing. The battle-scarred personality slowly unhinged his/her reptilian jaw and hissed this reply:
"Dreams *are* useless. Record them if you must and then put them away in a dresser."

Considering that a writing technique of mine had just been mocked, I remained a gracious host and directed zero anti-aircraft artillery fire to the pterodactyl. I let the comment slide — in other words. I later confided to the perplexed dream-writing student, that it was a "matter of culture — and post-modernism. Products from The Schools of Antiquity have severe cases of astigmatism."

"In the gradual darkness our conversation centers on Northern Lights: celestial messengers in green atomic oxygen, highlighted by red — the color of our impending nuclear demise."

"Their purpose is to apprise us of the Aurora Borealis, and how such lights will bring the true end."

One Meskwaki prophecy warns when the Northern Lights reach across the skies and touch the southern horizon, a great world war will ensue, causing an end to all life.

In two imaginary situations — the final "Flag War" and "Nuclear Winter"— I incorporate this omen.

/ / /

"As fiery sparks begin to materialize on an overturned skillet, the caterpillars stop."

This "sparks" theme is taken from childhood when Louise Stabs-me-in-the-Back, my aunt, used to prepare *be ko te*, biscuit, for the family. I would kneel beside the fire and wait anxiously until the cooking was done. Louise would turn the skillet over, knowing I would watch in fascination as sparks crisscrossed the hot skillet's surface. "Somewhere right now," she would say, "there must be a war." In my mind I saw brave "spark" soldiers come out in the raging battle to drag away their wounded comrades.

The First Dimension of Skunk, Nothing Could Take Away the Bear-King's Image, & *A Woman's Name is in the Second Verse* — "Claremont," "San Gabriel Mountains," "Orozco's murals in Frary Hall," and "Smiley Hall," are places and recollections taken from two academic years at Pomona College in Southern California where this Journey of Words began.

Wa Ta Se Na Ka Mo Ni, Vietnam Memorial — Theoretically, according to my father, Leonard Young Bear, the only person who can compose a Meskwaki Veterans song is a fellow Meskwaki veteran. The first time I heard this statement, it made a lot of sense. Proper representation was obviously a factor, as was experience.

There had been occasions before, however, when I wanted to make such a word-song. For months I contemplated the process of making a heart-stirring melody, punctuated with appropriate lyrics, names, and circumstances. There could be no greater tribute toward a tribal member, I recited, than someone who saw war firsthand, survived the ultimate horror, and came home.

But like the many things we plan to do in our lifetimes, the song never got past being an intention.

In 1982 when *Tri-Quarterly* magazine inquired if I could write about the Vietnam Memorial in Washington, D.C. I already had a good idea what to say. Basically, there are beautiful songs of tribute from the Grandfather World that can only be heard by those whose journeys never brought them back home.

/ / /

Three Translated Poems for October
(Draft to second poem)

Now that the autumn season has started,
I no ki - e we bi - ta qwa ki ki
one suddenly realizes
ko qwi - mi na we ne ta bi
the act of living goes fast
be ma te si we ni - e ne tti ya ska ki.
Ka bo ti ke a be - i ni
e tti ke ki - e me no ka mi i ke:
e ski ba kya te ki - ne tti ya ske i
Ne swa bi ta ka - ni swi
a ta swi be bo ne ya ni.

Me si kwe ti ye - ta ta ba ko ni
Box elder leaves
ba ba kwa se no ni - na i na - e we bi - me si kwi i ki
(break free in the wind as the sleet starts.

Or: break away when the icy rain starts)
E me tti se ki - ma ni - me te qwi

303

As the tree is now — out in the open,
stands there a man, who can be seen.
Ne ma so wa - i na - ne ni wa - ne wa bi.

While a good portion of these poems were originally "thought out" in Meskwaki, literary-related considerations were obviously involved. The draft above shows how things went and what was ultimately decided in terms of direction, content, message, and its translation.

It is an aspiration to one day compose everything in Meskwaki — the way it is supposed to be, free of intrusive novelties. I set this difficult goal for myself because Meskwaki is first and foremost the language I learned to communicate with, a language that drew clear diagrams of my exact place on earth via philosophy, cosmogony, and spirituality.

My grandmother believes we have each been born with an existential purpose; mine is the lifetime study of two languages.

What is thought of in the modern sense as contemporary Native American poetry is for me a distant form of storytelling. The main difference stems from the fact that English is adopted (in one way or another, frequently without a choice in the matter) and adapted as the primary linguistic medium. Therefore, the poetry that is written in English and the old/new tribal stories that are spoken in Meskwaki are two different things entirely.

While I am very much a layman when it comes to the Meskwaki lexicon, I am fortunate that I belong to an age-set who can *at least,* speak, think, and offer a semblance of written Meskwaki.

Certainly, the Journey of Words is far from being over.

Two Poems for Southeastern Washington — "Bullchild" and "Moon-woman" is in reference to the late Percy Bullchild's story of pre-Blackfeet origins found in *The Sun Came Down*, Harper & Row. To avenge the death of her secret lover — Snakeman — Moonwoman is forever in pursuit of Creator Sun and their seven sons, The Big Dipper.

Emily Dickinson, Bismarck and the Roadrunner's Inquiry — "I would be out of place in the tundra or desert, hunting moose for its meat and hide, tracking roadrunners for their feathers" is in reference to the Algonquin-speaking tribes of Canada and Northeastern Mexico. Variations of the Algonquin language are spoken on the North American continent by the Cree, Blackfeet, Chippewa, Kickapoo, Mexican-Kickapoo, Sauk, and Meskwaki Tribes — to name a few.

Meskwaki Tribal Celebration Songs — These traditional songs are included in a February 27, 1987 audio recording of the Woodland Drum Group produced by Canyon Records, 4143 North 16th Street, Phoenix, AZ 85106. The singers, including Stella and I, are from the Meskwaki (Red Earth) Tribal Settlement of Central Iowa.

THE ROCK ISLAND
HIKING CLUB

THE ROCK ISLAND HIKING CLUB

Symbolically, they stand close together
as they have done throughout their lives
on the Black Eagle Child Settlement. They peer
nervously into the canvas-shaded bigtop where
the tribal celebration is about to take place:
Mary Two Red Foot in her brilliant
cotton-white skirt has her one-year-old,
big-boned grandson, Robert No Body, slung
on her back in a green yarn-fringed shawl.

In the choking humidity, the serrated trim
of the tent vibrates as a concert bass drum
is being tuned. Mary squints in the harsh
daylight and begins talking: *"A kwi ma ka ski
bi ta bi ya ni ni-tte na-ki tta bi wa ki.*
I can't see in there, but they're already
seated." All she can make out are silhouettes
of singers on bales of hay.

Her younger half-sister, Doreen Half Elk,
with unseen hands on hips leans over
and listens intently. In the heat all Doreen
wishes to show is her face. A black and gray-
striped shawl covers her body and head.
Even her feet and shoes are in the dark
shade of her ruffled skirt. She's a statue
whose base is the earth.

Beside them, sitting in a semi-circle
on the ground, four white men in neckties,
suspenders, and straw hats are having lunch.
The baby, No Body, looks down at the men
who are nearly transparent in the hot,
July 15, 1932, sun.

OUR BIRD AEGIS

An immature black eagle walks assuredly
across a prairie meadow. He pauses in mid-step
with one talon over the wet snow to turn
around and see.

Imprinted in the tall grass behind him
are the shadows of his tracks,
claws instead of talons, the kind
that belongs to a massive bear.
And he goes by that name:
Ma kwi so ta.

And so this aegis looms against the last
spring blizzard. We discover he's concerned
and the white feathers of his spotted hat
flicker, signaling this.

With outstretched wings he tests the sutures.
Even he is subject to physical wounds and human
tragedy, he tells us.

The eyes of the Bear-King radiate through
the thick, falling snow. He meditates on the loss
of my younger brother—and by custom
suppresses his emotions.

AMERICAN FLAG DRESS

You know, my father, Willy Potato, and his cousin,
Jason Scarmark, are known throughout Iowa.
They came back from World War I as highly
decorated heroes. Newspaper clippings
from the *Des Moines Chronicle* were kept
under glass at the Tama County courthouse.
These we were allowed to view once a year
during the field trip taken by Weeping
Willow Elementary. While the courthouse
collections were housed ten miles away,
the tarnished medals and wrinkled ribbons
always had an effect on us even when they
seemed so far away—like stars. Letters
of honor received by the Potato Cousins
were read to us by teachers, and we
were astounded by photographs of how
they smiled with arms interlocked years ago
amid the burning fields, twisted armor, and death.

We were told that when trouble in Northern Europe
resurfaced, the Potato Cousins made news again
for volunteering their services to America.
But the gallant offer was politely denied.
From this unwavering act of courage many
an immigrant heart was stirred. And so when
the teenage sons of white farmers enlisted in
record numbers from the surrounding counties,
the Potato Cousins were credited for instilling
a fervid sense of patriotism.
Once when a journalist asked the cousins what
drove them to defend the country, my father said:
"A kwi ma-me ta kwi-mi ka ti ya ki ni. I ni-ye to ki-
a tta wa i-e tta i wa ji-ne me tto e me na na ki.
We do not like to fight. Perhaps this is the way it was
for our grandfathers." The loose
translation was turned around to read:
"We like to fight—unlike our grandfathers."
They were soon in demand at county
celebrations and state fairs.

In exchange for "gas, food, and *no* lodging,"
the heroes would don Sioux, *A tta,* war bonnets
and woolen uniforms to march in parades.
I would accompany them—not having a choice
in the matter—as reigning princess of the Annual
Black Eagle Child Field Days. On the hottest
and most humid summer days I felt sorry
for them as they led the processions in tight
combat boots while the State Pork Queen
and her rosy-cheeked court rode in automobiles.
Myself included, but on the trunk, facing backward.
And following behind would be the King of the Hobos,
an ever-present celebrity. He sat on a tan horse next
to the town mayors and assorted dignitaries.
On the Hobo King's secret signal the half-intoxicated
men would crow like ragged roosters as they looked at
my exposed ankles and chapped shins.

Among them always would be the bald-headed
white prophet named Mark. Well-rounded and portly
in his foul-smelling buckskin and fur hat, Mark
would nervously rub his glistening forehead
by habit and produce toothpick-size rolls
of dirt. These unwanted gifts were tossed
to our feet like ritual before he would say,
"Long before there was Hitler I dreamt
of him, Willy." In disgust my father could
only grimace and joke in Indian to Jason about
the dirt toothpick-manufacturing fat man.
"Ne ki-me ko-e be ma te si ya ni-a kwi-ko i ye-
na na tti-ke ke ne ma ki ni-ma ni-ni a bi tti-
wi ne si tti. Mo ko ma na-ke e i ki-ma na!
As long as I've lived never have I known
anyone to be this dirty. And this is a white
person!"

The Black Eagle Child Doughboys were often
billed as the main attraction. The cousins would
march triumphantly to their own unique chant:
"Ma ni tta-ni a ne mi-i tti tti mo ya kwi
Germany *na i na-ma na na kwi!* This is the way

our voices will sound when we attack Germany!"
When the march paused, they expertly removed
the long, gleaming bayonets from their rifles
and placed them in the scabbards without looking.
Then they'd take turns singing war dance songs
for each other on the deerhide drum made from
a quarter of a wooden barrel.

From April to September we traveled
to the cardinal points of Iowa, from Titonka
to Corydon and beyond, camping along
picturesque cliffs of the Mississippi,
or the green rolling banks of the water–
clouded–by–a–fleeing–Culture Hero's–foot
Missouri River. Wearing an American Flag
dress I would wave to the crowd with my
red-tailed hawk fan, and I became accustomed
to the ugly, sky-reflecting marble eyes
                              of the white children.
With blond disheveled hair they rolled over
the cobblestone streets mimicking death
from flint-tipped arrows. If they came close
enough where I could actually see my bright
reflection, I'd spit.

In the bizarre pretense we were allied against
a common Teutonic threat, one could say I barely
justified everyone's existence and survivability—
a living, breathing Statue of Liberty . . .

THE AURA OF THE BLUE FLOWER THAT IS
A GODDESS

Immediately after the two brothers entered
the Seafood Shoppe with their wide-eyed wives
and extra-brown complexioned stepchildren,
the shrimp scampi sauce suddenly altered
its taste to bitter dishsoap. It took a moment
to realize the notorious twosome were "carrying"
medicines, and that I was most likely the next
target in the supernatural shooting gallery.
It was yet another stab at my precious
shadow, *ne no ke we ni,* the one who
always Stands First, wildly unafraid
but vulnerable.

This placement of time, this chance meeting
at Long John Silver's had already been discussed
over the burning flower clusters, approved,
and scheduled for a divine assassination.
What an ideal place to invisibly send forth
a petraglyph thorn to the sensitive
and unsuspecting instep I thought.
Out of fear I had to spit out the masticated
crustacean into the folded Dutch bandana.
I signaled Selene with my eyes:
something is terribly wrong here.

Even in the old stories, *ke ta - atti mo na ni,*
my grandmother recited there was always
disagreement, jealousy, and animosity
between supernatural deities. That
actuality for humans, *me to se na ni wa ki,*
however was everpresent. It didn't conclude
as an impasse that gave us the weather,
the four seasons, the stars, sun, and moon.
Everything that was held together.

Unfortunately,

there could only be one re-creation
of earth. If it was requested in the aura
of the blue flower that I die,
the aura would make sure I die. . . .

Later, the invisible thorn—when removed by
resident-physicians (paying back their medical
loans)—would transform into some unidentifiable
protoplasm and continue to hide in the more
sensitive, cancer-attracting parts of the fish-
eater.

In the mythical darkness that would follow
the stories the luminescent mantle of the kerosene
lamp would aptly remind me of stars who cooled
down in pre-arranged peace—to quietly wait
and glow.

FATHER SCARMARK—WORLD WAR I HERO—AND DEMOCRACY

The black uncombed wig with stiff grotesque braids
sits atop his broad and pockmarked forehead;
and his grip on the dull tomahawk is almost woman-
like. Yes, Father Scarmark's winsome eyes
and slouched spine do not befit a proven warrior.
But the beaded American Flag designs on the bayonet
scabbard symbolize breaths stolen from German officers.
Back then he was called Master Check because he made
sure captured officers died mysteriously from minor
wounds during pauses in the artillery fire.

Today Father Scarmark is a chronic worrier; his tears
radiate eerily from the inside corners of his eyes.
He says he can vividly recall trench warfare.
We have been taught to distinguish that each
campaign has its own unique choking emanation.
But we have yet to understand what the Foggy
Dawn revealed: measurements of sanity?
And the eviscerated remains of young,
unsuspecting adversaries? He knows other
far more gruesome elements, as does his family.
They know the intimate details through the crude
odor that sometimes surfaces from the dilated pores
of his sweaty body.

And the long johns under his old-time dance outfit
are fiery red. In his armpit, almost hidden by
the mirrored arm bustles, is the Bible he helped
translate into our mother's tongue. They say
Scarmark's resurrection and pathologic vengeance
began when he was taken prisoner. This was early on.
There are stories he was maimed at parties of the German
echelon. Others say he was kept alive on boiled rats.

Fate arrived one afternoon as he was attempting
suicide. An artillery round landed above the bunker

at the exact moment he hanged himself. In the fiery
dust that followed, as the crudely fashioned noose
locked in tight braid-increments around his neck,
a page from *Tti-tte-sa,* Jesus, floated toward him
like a harmless moth and remained stationary,
long enough for him to read about the criminals
who were nailed beside Christ. Once he begged
for his Forgiveness, the rope loosened itself
and rose mysteriously to the ceiling and burned
in the shape of a crucifix. Although the fire
went out, its ethereal shape was imprinted
in the European air.

Today "Father J. Scarmark"—as his name reads
on the deteriorating mission door—had this phantom
transfiguration painted on the church.
"Ma ni ke-mi ne kwi ya ni-be ma te si we ni.
This is what gave me my life" is the painting's title.
It is marveled at by the few daring white people
who stop at the mission on their sightseeing scurry
through the Settlement.

Although he speaks in repetitions and clichés,
Father Scarmark gets incensed if family members
mock his unoriginality. Under the grotesque black
wig, his family recited, "should be stamped
"Boastful War Hero." Yet few in the tribe can
match his deeds. Over supper he is known to say:
"I ni ye to ki-we tti-mi ya ne ne mi ya tti.
E we ta se i ya ni. That is probably the reason
they are jealous of me. Since I am a proven
veteran. *A kwi ke-e ma ma to mo na ni we ya ni.*
And not because I am a religious man."
But the male heirs knew differently.
Especially Scarmark the Second.

"Bravery in war has nothing to do with it,"
he once told his brothers who always
held his judgments in reserve.
But he went on and they listened
to the shrewd history of Black Eagle Child

politics: it was their father who formed
the 1923 Business Council after tampering
with the ballot boxes. At issue was democracy—
the one-person, one vote concept. Unfortunately,
their father's father had raped and murdered
a young woman, Dorothy Black Heron;
and the county authorities offered to forget
the crime if the Scarmark patriarch agreed
to become a federally recognized Chief
and allow education into the tribe.
When their father saw his father step
perfectly into his own moccasin tracks,
at the scene, there was no choice but
to burn the pivotal vote.

From there on out, American Indians
as practicing Democrats and Republicans
became a literal myth. That single,
incinerated vote, as would be seen by scholars
later on, initiated the arduous rock-strewn
journey toward our demise. Every jagged edge
stabbed our sensitive feet and we became
hobble-legged. Mandatory education
for tribal youth was enacted by the state
of Iowa at the expense of "Heron Dorothy Black."
Often their father would openly reflect (long before
the sons could fathom the implications of the story)
that had the election swung for sacred, traditional
chieftainship the "Cigarstore Indian" days
would have returned. It was well known most
youth fled to the hills in short-lived protest.
When food and water supplies were depleted
they came out to federal truant officers
who patiently herded them to the barn stalls
for the wicked and cultural disfiguring.

THE REPTILE DECREE FROM PARIS

What could my one-armed grandfather, Victor Bearchild,
possibly be presenting to the Caucasian visitor
named Subchief? (In elementary I used thick
ugly tablets by that same name.) It doesn't look
like any kind of "Trophy" as the label notes.
It's not a silver-plated rendition
of basketball players or runners in miniature
on the fireplace mantel. First appearances
through the magnifying glass indicate
the speckled hide of some animal,
covering the visitor's pale hand
and Victor's sleeve-knotted half arm;
and in the blurred background is a maple
sapling in front of a whitewashed house.
A closer look reveals the open beak
of a predator bird whose wingfeathers
have been trimmed into spikes, with serrated
edges. Several loose feathers are entwined
around the uncommon combination
of the animal-bird's torso.

In my grandfather's good left hand
is a paper document that has been folded
so much sections hang on weakly by creased
corners only. Can we zoom in on his "left"
and then down? In front of his hefty shoes
is a tin box—approximately eight by ten inches—
where important items were stored.
The bird's screaming face and its
speckled ally must have protected
the contents with supernaturalism
from those curious enough to pry.
And there would be loose stones
that rattled and rumbled against the walls
of the box like distant earth tremors,
a mystical alarm that woke both owner
and sentinel.

My Woodlands people, having adopted
the alphabet in the 1600s, often kept
communiqués from Great Britain, Spain,
and France. These mats or "scrolls"
were considered valuable expressions
of other "Man," and tribal keepers
passed these indecipherable symbols
from one generation to the next.
Some contained signatures of distant
Kings and Queens, including their wax seals
and ribbons. If the scroll had a story that
could be remembered as having a history-making
role where sacred aid was conjured, it became
part of the clan altar.

In the 1930s, however, when anthropologists
were allowed to translate one scroll
we were apprised it was a decree from
a King in Paris, ordering our "total
extermination. Leave not a single limb
intact, for this race can regenerate
itself back to life like reptiles."
Why? the elders expressed meekly.
Because the trading toll your grandfathers
demanded from tribes and foreigners
passing through your territories,
related Dr. Culsax in the kerosene-lit
interior of the earth lodge, was deemed
"unreasonable and highly insulting."
The Reptile Decree eventually drove us
south from Wisconsin into Illinois,
then Kansas in exile, and finally here—
to Iowa.

Jesus, this photo could be that very scroll!
It's not any prize then.
With that as confirmation I begin to align
the sunlight through the glass and burn
minute holes in the emulsion and grain,
hoping the fiery light will reach
the jewel-clustered fingers

of ancient royalty, transgressing
time: someone's offensive decision.
I wholly deny and retract all prayers
it listened to and received in error—
centuries of misery. Joseph Campbell,
punch "Esc." The software of mythologic
understanding dissolves.

Looking again I notice the knee portion
of my grandfather's trousers bulging out,
even as he stands erect. The imprint
of his kneecaps is solid, like evidence
of—too much sitting? But he's middle-aged,
and he was never idle. Hell, he was a bloody
wood-carver! (The "phantom knee" effect
is a tribal term which refers to clothes
that accumulate dirt and grease from constant wear.
The joke being, the clothes will come to life
whenever the ignorant owner decides to take
them off. The mere association embarrasses me.
My own grandfather, of all people.)
It isn't that he was too lazy to dress for company;
it is probably because he only had two pairs
of trousers. Of course. And there was no
laundry soap that week in 1934 when the bird-
animal entity was rudely awakened by the harsh
sunlight—without ample warning from stones,
or an earth tremor. No appointment was made,
Dear Charlevoix.

JANUARY GIFTS FROM THE GROUND
SQUIRREL ENTITY

It can go beyond the case of wild, little animals
storing dozens of Black Eagle Child beans and acorns
(two sizes) in conspicuous places throughout the trailer.
Winter is an impetus, obviously, but there's a strong
suspicion that the beans and acorns found between
our towels, clothes, and footwear are gifts
from deities who reside on this pinetree-lined
hillside. Since they cannot reveal themselves,
they probably appointed these intermediaries.
But the fact there are no fields or forests
that would bear these particular varieties
within a quarter-mile circumference makes
a sane and logical argument against ground
squirrels or mice making the storage trek
in a single night.

Before the performance trip to St. Mary's College
in Winona, Minnesota, I found eight shiny acorns
in my Reebok tennis shoes, the pair I would have worn
for driving, not the ones I use under theatre lights.
It was definite I'd use them. And Selene found
gray, brittle ones in her sewing machine in compart-
ments that could not have been opened by any creature.
Strangely, the year before that, before leaving for Taos,
our favorite wine glasses were filled to the brim
with beans called *bi ya*.

I've also theorized the gifts are paybacks
from grateful chipmunks who grew fat last summer
on commodity surplus peanuts, the ones I fed them
as they appeared on the log pile in the yard,
facing the earthlight for the first time
with miniature black eyes. But all is contradicted
by the memory of a Grandfather who owned a tin
antique suitcase filled mysteriously with acorns
he said must have been brought by mice.
No one ever had the audacity to ask:

How could they gnaw through metal?

And just recently when I saw walnuts fall
from an overhanging oak limb and land precisely
in the four corners of a satin-lined casket
of the woman I was paying my respects to,
I had to rethink the whole scenario.
There was my blind uncle, you see,
in the dream about "The Bread Factory"
that came to mind.

THE MASK OF FOUR INDISTINGUISHABLE THUNDERSTORMS

It is the thunderstorm
                    at first
that begins speaking
            from an easterly direction
We listen to its vociferous
                    non-threatening
voice and fall asleep

This weather doesn't care
                    to know itself
our inner physical journals
record

We assess: icy rain is no different
            than wet branch-breaking
snow and the summer deluge
                    that stretches
toward autumn combines all into one
            haunting answer

That of a wintry inevitability
                    glazed ice
over the terrain
            The symphony

Before awakening we hear clouds
that quietly explode
            from within
Watery moonlit fragments hit
            the roof
            saying: in the case of anger
fist-sized hail would splinter
                    everything

The woodlands horizon
is therefore portrayed as a jagged

            lavender line
and encircled in yellow
                      obviously
is the sun
             reducing humankind
to spherical dimensions
                        making
known the presence
of duality

That the Black Hummingbirds
are saviours as well as
assassins

                    / / /

Grandmother Earth
sits with her bare razor-nicked
back towards you
                      the observer
the would-be infringer
            the one who taps out
salvation messages with a silver
surgical instrument

Her daughter's precious son
            she recognizes
But the blood-letting is deceptive
What was supposed
                  to be seasonal
self-purification appears through
            ultrasound
as a protoplasmic thorn
carved with indecipherable
                      petroglyphs

                    / / /

We swear nothing is apocalyptic
while garish beacons from
            the tribal gaming complex

create apparitions
in the sky

Balanced on top a floating mass
            of ourselves
under the guidance of an ochre
                    seal-eyed
word-collector in a tight
flannel shirt
            hole-ridden jeans
and Presbyterian church-donated
            shoes
we cradle fine shovels
that are designed to slice
            the earth
leaving behind rectangular-
            shaped markings
of a former industrious
society

SUMMER TRIPE DREAMS
AND CONCRETE LEAVES

1.

There exists a future when green trees will be extinct.
In our ingenuity artificial tree factories—ATFS—
        will flourish

Far ahead I see myself walking under one,
and I grow uneasy at the thought of chunks
of painted concrete swaying in the man-made
breeze from bark-textured iron rods.

Don't worry, says the regional safety inspector,
they can withstand mega-knot winds.
Plus they've got internal warning mechanisms
with stress signals link to monolithic fans
in the western part of the state. Should a fracture
occur, the fans are automatically programmed
to slow down.

Bullshit, I think as white dust and chips
of paint blow about in the false wind,
stippling my indolent face.

2.

Inside the honeycomb-lined tripe intestine
there is a woman held captive, and I am there with her.

She resembles Debra Winger, the Hollywood actress.
She sits on my lap undressed and allows me to explore
her smooth virginal skin, her sensuousness.
Outside of her bone frame and beyond the newborn,
translucent skin, she cries. Together we hear herself.

The fine design on the walls and the terraced floors

begin to tremble. One end of the floor begins to surge
like an ocean wave and it travels beneath—
and lifts us upward, speeding toward
consciousness.

EAGLE FEATHERS IN COLOUR PHOTOCOPY

Edgar Bearchild uses modern non-electric tools
to make duplicates of his grandfather's feather boxes,
and while he can easily find 1920s-style jewelry
and brass mirror cases at flea markets for decorative
                    inlay, the museums by law
can only buy eagle feathers in colour photocopy,
for the American symbol for freedom faces
extinction. Again. So before setting out on
Interstate 35 North to St. Euripides,
                    Edgar places these facsimiles
in the hollowed-out portion of oblong board
and treats them as his predecessors did, keeping
them enclosed and therefore dry between lightweight
wood until the moment needed in either Black Eagle
        Child prayer, combat, or sorcery.

"They almost look real . . . if you look real close
squinting one eye," remarks the Asian-looking
curator with the faux Armani suit and butch
haircut. Edgar thinks a proper reply might entice
                    a sale, but he panics
in not knowing the curator's gender. He pops
the brass compact open and sees the two of them
in the mirror, together. One androgynous, the other
with hope. *Neither of us, because of our slender-*
                    shaped eyes, really
have to squint that much, was what he wanted
to say. The curator and a tribal staff member
wink at each other. Only then the Gothic
eyeshade. She nods, winces in cancerous
                    agreement, and dictates:
"Ethnoforms Project: Black Eagle Child
Featherbox Maker, Edgar Bearchild of Central
Iowa, entitled, 'No. 4029, My Summer at Fortune
Lodge, Alaska.'"
Like a capricious a judge at a cattle show that
had just slapped his rear with a blue ribbon,
Ed's rear shinnied. "Why Fortune, and did

you go there?" she asked. I once sensed
                    a murderer there,
or its Anchorage victim knew something about
that place. Her Leica eyes mechanically blinked,
urging him to elaborate. He held up the lid
of the wooden box: covered under
            beveled glass, matboard,
and brass screws, a 4 by 16 inch relief
sculpture on catlinite of a pointy-eared dog
knelt Sphinx-like at the end of a pipestem.
"$4,029.00, and the flute-pipe is included?"
            Yes, twice. This blindfolded
figure on the Lazy-Boy is a self-portrait.
Over the keys my fingers are held in musical
suspension, while the Swirling Red Arrow
is gourd-rattle conceived. Assessing
                events quickly, the arrow
draws a blue, wavy horizon, like that
ocean where the killer whale swims,
half-surfacing. Thus, within its faraway body
names, addresses, letters, and numbers,
            are delineated. And only that.
Behind the dog's neck swirls of smoke
are being emitted from the bowl of the pipe,
Sherlock Holmes that I am.

THE BREAD FACTORY

The tribal bread factory is missing,
as well as the pigfeet-canning operation.
And the light-complexioned, physically
challenged woman, the one who controlled
the giant stainless steel tumbler, knows why.
Mystery solver that Lisa Jean is.

Above, over the green rounded hill,
my catatonic uncle strikes the partially
embedded walnuts with his hooked cane.
This is a testament, he reports, to the stars
that fell overnight in legions. Like large
chunks of hail that have just landed,
the walnuts pop up and roll away.

Lured by indiscernible words
I follow behind meekly, a servant
about to be entombed. In my hand
a dark wooden bowl. Beneath the greasy
dish towel there are more walnuts and many
are cracked, dusty, and dry. (Later, through
the Ground Squirrel, there would be acorns.)

"So wha''bout your dream-ma 'bout paranormal
golf?" complained the mystery-solving woman.
With clinking leg braces and crutches she
hobbled toward me. In a breath of vanilla
extract and worry she said, "Mine dealt with a water-
less aquarium filled with newborn ground hogs.
An educator then advised me to pour in a half
cup of water to prolong their life."

Beside her tall sister, Lisa Jean kneaded
the dough over the flour-covered table.
Wrists she slashed every summer were visible.
When the raised scar tissue was accidentally
brushed, an eyelid tick ensued. As she leaned
forward in her beige flower print dress,

331

engrossing herself in work, I visualized
a shameful thought—a phantasmagoric
union between us. Long elegant legs
in black knit socks behind splints
of chrome steel. . . .

A SEASON OF PROVOCATION AND OTHER ETHNIC DREAMS

1.

It began near the site
of a smoldering but vacant
mobile home. East Quail
Road. There, blared the scanner,
relatives conveyed a teenager
was upset for being deprived
of a "real Three Stooges
videotape." Thus was the sky
ignited. Next, through the jet's
window, I waved to my wife,
Selene Buffalo Husband,
as the bus-like craft turned
over a runway of corn stalk
stumps. And then we ascended,
westward. Unbuckled I sat in
the back and stretched my arms
across the tops of a soft bench.
Standing beside me, an ethnic
pilot was uneasy. He deflected
my questions with stares toward
earth of concern. Like an amateur
verbal boxer I recited: "Best to leave
a rock that refuses to talk alone;
best just to listen to the water
rippling around it."

2.

Once, after an all-night drive
to Taos, New Mexico, I became
disoriented. At some plaza square,
perhaps close to the designated
meeting place with the poetry
reading contact, I approached

a group of ethnics on a balcony
and, thinking they were other
invited poets, asked: "Are you
here to meet Peter Cottontail?"
Unflinchingly, while wiping salad
bits from their mouths, they pointed
to each other. "No, but we have bugs
Bunny here—and, oh, here's Daffy!"
Travel-faced in their expensive sun-
glasses I was convex at the ethnologic
query about who I was. Sí, I said, an
Indio, from a nearly immiscible history.
Years later, I recall this exchange
and wonder if Woody Woodpecker
really has a daughter and what
her name might be. Is it Splinter?
you knothead. Methinks it's a clue
from Oklahoma via the Lazy-Boy
quest sessions in the disappearances
of Lauria and Ashley.

3.

English for Black Eagle Childs,
Pat "Dirty" Red Hat once noted,
is saturated with linguistic pitfalls.
For example, he once asked
a coy waitress at an old German-
style restaurant on Interstate 80,
"Do you serve alcoholics?"
"Yes, we do," he was told
that Sunday morning. At a Sears
auto garage the manager peace-
signed when Pat asked about
"hallucinogenic" rather than
halogen headlights. And at
the Youth Services Facility
co-workers oft-reflected when
he "applied a Heineken" on
a muskmelon pulp-choking
girl. That singular misapplication

had more notice than the turbulent
adolescence saved. But no one quipped
at the line given when he mis-dressed
himself: "I am completely reverse
of what I am." Because that term
could fit anyone, ethnic—
or otherwise.

FOR LAZY-BOYS, DEVOTED PETS, HEALTH, AND TRIBAL HOMELAND REALITY, OR HOW WE ARE EACH A LONE HOVERCRAFT

Deceived by
autumn dust
movement that would've
brushed daylight
from the Lazy-Boy
was expended
needlessly

*

Polar Bear
"the Nicole S. Special"
aligns its Akita profile
in the small clear
spot on the window
where frost has been
scraped
reminding me
that even *he*
is important
as "Won-ton"
my fiction(al)
editor

*

Life I like
said my brain
to its unabashed
self but a back-
ache? *No* re-
sounded a reply
that set off
from within
a soundless

336

fire alarm fashioned
from sculpture
remnants
of pulsating
nerve endings
making Milky
Way the after-
flash of the
Creator's blink
throughout my
universal
physicality

*

Bear your letters
fish without eyes
drift in currents
embedded in soil

Crows are tossed
in black clusters
by the windshield
wipers

*

Every morning
this spring is without
my younger brother's
massiveness

No red wagon
with three round-
faced children coming up
the muddy driveway
nearly toppling

No massiveness
No eternity
in 1995

POEMS FOR DREAMS AND UNDERWATER PORTALS

1.

Behind Selene and Javier Buffalo Husband
the wooded river valley emits a resilient
green-yellow glow. From earth's
supernatural seam bubbles in twin
forms surface, erasing with their color
of eminence that transfixed sense
called Normalcy.

2.

Quiet singing summer,
quiet singing summer.

Within the swan dance
formation, though, two
with young are not typical.
Especially when one
newborn refuses to release
the cut-beaded handle
of a fan. Hers. Then
the green snow cone
becomes an issue.

Like an accident-bound
train, the dancers brake
and collect themselves
in a timely sigh. When
the drum's rumble—
a signal—is softened,
they go backward.
Summer singing
quietly.

3.

Without legs the elongated,
round back of a wooden chair
rests in a ditch. Discarded.
Next, a young woman wearing
a yellow house-cleaning glove that
is vertical appears. Before the corner
of a star quilt lands perfectly in my palm,
waking me, I hoist my arm like a flag:
Was that Ashley Judd?

4.

Through certain readings
of old documents that visually
self-translate, we influence the sunlight
to assume triangle-shaped machinations.
Here the purple ink is Animistic.
Over the wind-trampled prairie grass
where the small lodges glistened
under the all-sky flashes,
we sang: Risk. Risk. And then
two more for assurance
in a non-human domain.

NOVEMBER 12, 1951

"Literary expression,"
Edgar Bearchild once noted,
"is a sadistic mutation of the genes
of intelligence—on my father's side—
that I was unjustly deprived of."

IMPROVISED SEALANT FOR HISSING WOUNDS

Crumpled clothes on a Lazy-Boy
recliner. This chair is the source
that shapes vague or distinct
pictures behind my smoky
blindfolded eyes. But there
are other things, too, like a basin
plug that clicks and attracts
me to its trademark: "Alley."
So now this is a phantasm,
forming beyond cedar-shadow,
a visitor—a summation
for the Navigator.

In a room beset with faint light:
A jogging suit, baseball cap,
sunglasses, and Dr. Crockston
who's under sedation for
keeping a secret via slow
death by alcohol.

There's no space in his
physiology to make amends
to Facepaint who died from
complications of sharpened
screwdrivers. "The Doc" was
there with the first Black Eagle
Child Settlement cross-dressers.
In his raspy breathing I sense
a conspiracy coming
through the duct tape
sarcophagus: He, too,
will become a mute,
inaccessible shadow
unless the significance
of "15 air waves
tickets" can be deciphered.

AN ACT OF PURIFICATION, NO. 1

"Normalcy," wrote Bearchild
in *The Black Eagle Child Journals*,
"is an acquisition that dresses
itself in rigorous yet unassailable
forms of temerity." But when
the tall metal ladder covered
itself with a cross child's frosty
handprints, the Recall petition
for one *bo ki te ba* or hole-in-
the head was promptly cleansed
with braided strips of smoky,
ethnobotanic persuasion. There
was, after all, the lunatic social
worker who preyed on troubled
clientele at tribal cemeteries and
a brother whose house had been
 lightning-struck, setting fire to
stolen casino surveillance equipment.
And everything began "with a talking
Go-Kart ..."

FOUR POEMS FOR IMMEDIACY

1.

Selene Nicotine of Pinelodge Lake
forms herself from the icy night winds.
With hummingbird-like appendage
borrowed from a moth, her surfboard
is invisible.

Floating beside me I detect her
mythic scent, that of a reddish
orange flower, the pollen of which
coats her normal shoes, her
delicate underwings.

As a serpentine hold-out
I intermingle and then recoil
over the stippled concrete.
No one, I later whisper in
the daylight, shall hold anyone
accountable for the first case
of infidelity.

2.

In front of a house with
large windows a whirlwind
lifts while three others align
themselves to the west
in varying heights of descent,
waiting. Like a chiropractor,
my father adjusts to correctness
his face and torso, then steps
outside with an elder to beseech
the fury to calm. Under the closet
frame I clutch an unknown
baby and wince at the banging

wall, at the clenched fist
of a cookie called Massacre.

3.

Englebert Hubberdee,
the hound dog, relays
a thought as I close my
eyes beside the snowy
riverbank: Larger than
a pile of trash bags
there was a figure here.
We scan the tousled area.
Dry grass and deer bones,
oily mud over the frozen
earth, and ghostly fish
resonations.

4.

From under water a pair
of bright animal eyes glows.
Are you—am I right—
a divine sentry? Is this hole
in the tree a door to your
home? The answer
all along is your own:
A Supernatural owns
the submerged rat terrier,
within the phantasmagoric
tree they reside.

CRESTWOOD SCHOOL OF SOCIAL RESEARCH

1.

Perched atop the neon-outlined
towers of Crestwood's Rural Cooperative
the giant farm animal faces made
of chrome shimmer. Some, like the swans
and the llamas, are sculpted in German silver.
Depicted in their twisted torsos are their
commercial histories—of sleek hood
ornaments and ochre-stained sacrificial
offerings. Elaborate, they rotate like weather
vanes. Beside them, the Chance Rooster
        Neal breeds of Blue Heelers
are honored, along with the Francine
Choo-Choos and Spike Rusty Mow Mows.
Calibrated to perform every 35 minutes,
the town's notables resemble grotesques.
Displayed along the narrow Crew-C-Fix
Highway, their kinetic shadows stretch,
drifting across small valleys where the gravel,
another success factor, is chalky and lung-
abusive.

2.

As soon as tired eyes close, the air festers
with heinous intent. It's undeniable, so attests
the Swirling Red Arrow ally who motions *ghosts
relive horrific deaths here.* Within its restless
citizens they manifest themselves through eyes
that are silver and reflective, which divide them
into other personalities. From the recesses
of the famous gravel pits, the stories record,
shadow-swallowing serpents once possessed
        flags of Lost Nations.

Who owns who? thus sing the tan deities
of today as a warning—for you to surrender.
That's why their rattles replicate deathly whispers.
Whereas for us it was diamonds, hedonistic
occurrences within God's musical instruments.

3.

Disguised as a gravel pit and encircled by metallic
pendants strung on telephone wire—ten by twenty
square miles—visible only from the sky, the extra-
terrestrial processing station makes this place
ingenuous. For their road lost—it happens
to them, too—the fencepost signs give direction:
O-SO-E-Z reads the first; 2-B-B-Z the second;
SO GET LOST the third; and W/YR AUNT'S
FARM MILK the last.

Closer to the outskirts, Daizy, the Muddi Kow,
winks when her blue milk fills, vacates, and refills
her clear udders. Regular travelers exit I-35
to behold another vacation check-off:
As the electrolyte drains, her long rubber
eyelashes shake. Equally famous, the blue
butter impregnated with yellow cheese dots
is shipped worldwide. "Sticks of Blue, Packed
by Sue." Wearing a Dutch fisherman's cap,
            the Campbell Soupish model
waves its windmill arms to no one. Thereby
creating an access for mythic trickery, I think.
Not even a smelly animal's foot would deter
its quest to restore its vision, using the gray
corneas, the ones taken from you in a crude
ophthalmic surgery. No telltale forensic dye
would imply that the nerve-ending
was severely severed.

4.

After curious motorcycles roar by, I am wrapped
with green inquisitive stripes of light. "The King
of Spain," a lover of Old Bikes, would've delighted
at these contraptions of extreme synergism. For
this month only we are 59 years old. Our grand-
mothers raised us, so the revving of the engines
of the Ram-shaped Cruizers only saddens me.
To Thyself: Not even the monolithic fans
bringing the autumn breeze interest me.
          Starting from Ida Grove,
near the Buffalo Compounds, I began
missing Selene. Wedged against a Quick-Gal
(lon) bathroom corner and with the .380
Beretta unholstered, this is what I torment:
Tomorrow we'll argue over Nouns & Verbiage,
yes, delaying lessons on Cru-Cials & Other Necess's.
They're scheduled to integrate in one year? So I'm
humoured in Morose Levels, crowned racks of it.
Sauteed in sausage grease with snow peas,
mushrooms, ginger, soy sauce, and scallions
manyfold, these venison strips contain
nostalgic protein, memories from
the succulent spine. A soft touch
to the elbow of a dream.

DISH SHAPES AND REMNANT POOLS

High above, behind
the extended wings
of cranes, lavender
clouds flatten themselves
into a dish-shaped flotilla.
Heading East, they keep
one cautious space apart.
They would be useful,
I resolve, if they made
the mass of our anxieties
a less orderly horizon.

"That's what's coming,"
I voice-note. "Quick days—
remnant pools of floods,
reflecting indiscernible
choices." Suddenly,
the blue sky scrapes
itself against the forest
canopy of thorns.
From this contact,
premeditated, a giant
cottonwood fluff drifts
toward me crosswind.
Midway North, as if
in dream, a bubble-shape
alights near an uprooted
Box Elder. And then, acting
unwanted, the capricious
sphere rolls into the sweet-
smelling frost.

With the daylight disabled
and mending itself, a *realm-
slipping* event self-manifests:
In former juvenile hands, my
grandfathers' ledgers, which
were written in purple ink,

self-translate from tribal
syllabics to English. To read
inscription without knowing
equals the point where night
introduces daybreak through
the ecstatic songs of circling
geese. Before ruffling their
feathers in furtive ritual,
small swimmers gather
near the green, hollow
stem to re-define themselves.
Everyone dry-mud prepares
for this sensual elaboration,
this moment before autumn,
winter, You, memory-maker,
and the other seasons are issued
from the green, hollow stem—
a flute, as an eagle's
sequential whistles.

IN THE TREE'S SHADOW

My dog is as old as my bereavement.
The wooden red wagon dissolves
into the mossy ground. "Madnesse."

A one-cloud rain. Like wild architects
we seed the rough hill with grass.
By machine and wind, trees have fallen.

In the tree's shadow an orange light
holds the sunset's color. I don't question
this Animistic reaching. Of the growth
on the bark that shines.

MOON-LIKE CRATERS ON MY LEGS

Throughout my investiture
as a "word collector," there
were extraterrestrials disguised
as well-meaning Scandinavians.
You'd think they would've told
me. Stuff I should've known
about or expected, like rat-claw
messages on doors and other
supernatural revealings.

Except for a couple
of visits, there was
never any unfolding,
no alien-to-human
communiqués,
nothing to comport
their omnipresence
except suspected
implant movement.
"Twice, subepidermal
bullet-shaped devices
readjusted on forearms
for reception," I wrote.
"The side-effects consist
of physical extrusions,
like unhealing wounds
or toenails coming off,
regenerating."

Based on which body part
is most susceptible to injury,
the implants calculate where
to skin surface. Rash outbreaks
thus riddle my thighs with scar
tissue, confusing my Specialist.
"Periscopes," I tried to joke.
Finally, with fresh tissue
depleted, they relocated,

taking refuge in my toes.
At the slightest shoe
discomfort or a sun
deck sliver, the feet
suffer.

At least the podiatrist
watches *X-Files* something.
"In a swimming pool once,"
he lets me convey,
"I scraped my knee:
Via antibiotic bandages
the wound could hardly
recoup." Liquid immersion
interfered? "Yes." Chlorine?
"In Albuquerque." He listens
with keen indifference
as I recount our metabolic
and intuitive natures.
"But showers also
provide access to distant
acts of sexual depravity,
like that time I received
the Yosemite killer's
license plate letters
before his last life-
taking."

Another time, I ascertain,
in a drunken hallway scuffle
between lovers I got shin-kicked.
Accidentally. The device
reversed into the bone.
"There, the scar is crescent-
shaped and indented like moon
craters."

LARAMIE'S PERIPHERAL VISION

1.

Small, graceful hawks whose tailfeathers
are decorated with menacing upside-down
faces of ancient swordsmen hunt over
the green, wooded hillside.

A house, symbolically ours, is scheduled
to be built there, we're told—once politics
quell. Whenever that happens, we reply,
the tribal housing contract stipulates we'd
be mere "occupants." Maybe when Laramie
            gets out, offers the mother,
it'll be done? The father raped the tropical
stepdaughter. And that accounts for everything—
right? The world is pockmarked with holes,
son, like the dozens in your dad's freaking
head, King of the Coconuts.

It isn't an impediment, Selene
and I rationalize quietly, occupying
a casino-funded edifice. The sunlit window,
after all, will be the same. The door knobs,
however, will need replacing, likewise
the kitchen cabinets, air ducts,
            closet doors, ceiling,
and the water heater. If the unsealed
foundation doesn't crack, the frame may
last fifty years. So the oxymoron of having
waited five centuries for exclusive non-
ownership of a new house is tolerable. But
think of our matrilineal customs, how tribal
by-laws preclude women from such
benefits. Nothing—it seems—can ever be
reversed. But there's compromise. And
even precepts are subject to change,
times when they seemingly are no longer
tenable.

353

2.

To make it free from negativity
this paradoxical house will be blessed
by my father. Later, it'll be swept
for electronic bugs. Even after their
petition-ouster, the relics (rogue tribal
council operatives) remain bothersome.
            Their relatives now
stalk us, leaving hell's postcards—flares,
in our mailbox. For truckers' showers,
piglet farms, and stock car losers,
tribal sovereignty was waived. (If the Lazy-
Boy Navigator saw deceased relatives change
into geese, wrapping their necks around
the poles of the cosmic earth lodge,
arranging themselves into a message
on how to remove them, politically,
then it was necessary.)

Under "relic" reign, their mish-mash
consultants all named Lowell & Lowell
abated tribal direction. These Pathetics
wore unkempt silver feather earrings,
black dusters, and platinum toupees.
At the VIP rodeo section, they all
ate cups of chilled fruit topped with
whipped cream and arena dust.

Casino-obsessed, they also allowed
trespassers to kill the team-hunting hawks
rather than intervene, evicting them. And
when their own relatives' eyes began
missing the daylight, they were still
            stupid. The Deities,
it was theorized, disagreed with hypocrisy.
There's irony when Priests pray that any
Evil that's directed toward tribal homeland
Pogo-reverse itself. Sitting beside them,
the necro-verted tribal officials, their
own sons, vowing unsuccessfully

to avenge their perceived genetic
deficiencies. In sabotaging tribal
affairs, was it simply because
your Chihuahua relative
bedded their spouse-to-be
before mold with a single hair
grew on its inconspicuous nose?

3.

These empty but jet-streaked clouds
possess details of Laramie's metamorphosis
into a fatherless guitarist. Like the First Earth,
there's transgression and then consequence.
He'll awake, digesting a wide dispersal
of pernicious space. And he'll ask, as would
another, about the purpose of treeless valleys.
Maybe it'll be good, we predict holding Merlots,
him, undergoing therapy. (I knew my father
at ten; he lost his at thirteen. We are what, what
are we to each other—then?) Upon returning,
his petulant sisters will ignore their mother's
call over Rolling Head Valley. A resident-
shadow will flicker in his peripheral vision,
reminding him of Weeping Willow's
Halloween supplies: Court exhibit
photos of Wal-Mart bags crammed
into his closet, some with lollipop
handles sticking out, including
orange edible flutes and candy corn—
next to the poster of Traci Lords,
pre–*Melrose Place,* and purple
Reebok tennis shoes.

4.

On windy days, the hawks agree to catch
invisible currents, spiraling upward until
they vanish in the afterburn-streaked skies.

Self-assessment is triggered:
That's how I am sometimes. The group task
set aside, like a mortuary custom that doesn't
belong or is poorly conceived. The hawks
will leave to survive, whereas my morbid
victimization thrives. Soon, I expect Caterpillars
to scoop out the reddish brown sand. Above
this hollowed-out hillside, I whisper to Selene,
is where we'll recoup the sound of silverware
clinking against dishes, children's laughter,
life discussion, and where the furniture goes.
My last breath is therefore irrelevant.
Inasmuch as my grandmother took
care of me, including others,
I'll seek the same.

MANIFESTATION WOLVERINE

FOUR HINTERLAND ABSTRACTIONS

1.

today a truck
carrying a tomahawk
missile reportedly tipped
over on the interstate
       somewhere
labeled an "unarmed warhead"
its fabulous smoke had to be
placated with priest-like
words being murmured by
      yucca-wielding
authorities & while covering
the dormant but cross entity
with tarps that had paintings
of blue mountaintop lakes
    they affirmed
their presence with nudges
& reminders this valley
was sculpted by the once-lovely
wings of a vulture & here
    is where
you will quietly attend to
the disorder we heard plainly
over the traffic's ubiquitous
din & before a smoldering
      star's song

2.

from one winter night
an inquisitive firefly has directed
itself toward my three children
& through its testament
    of cold light
floral patterns appear over
their snowy tracks replacing
shadows with light that's detailed
& compelling us to place ourselves

        beside the weeping
willow grandfather to ask him
please behold the witness
        witness

3.

previously as a winsome
ghost that's awash in green
& yellow pulsating colors
it taunted the blue heeler
        named
simon simone ese'who lunged
thereafter fish-like into the night
arcing its scaled torso in order
to bite the protoplasmic wings
        so make note
of this psychically-attuned
defender i scratched on
the frosted car window
without looking around

4.

on a hot windy afternoon in
downtown why cheer he walked
across the street from where
the dime store used to be
        pointing
to a remnant column he said
ke me kwe ne ta ayo a be i yo e te ki?
do you recall what used to be here?
having just arrived from
        overseas
& wearing boots covered
with ochre grains of distant
battlefields he reached down
& crushed several into small
        clouds
that sped over the sidewalk
as i nodded yes

FROM THE LANDSCAPE:
A SUPERIMPOSITION

1.

Silhouetted against the snowy outskirts
of the Chelsea township, the Black Coyote
    is cool as it prances
over aisles of cornfield stubble. Seeing
this divine guard, traveling parallel
    and disappearing,
erases symbolisms of rapacity
previously held. Then, as I mentally
    compose a song
for Wolverine, its gangly portrait
reappears—and it's superimposed
    over a maple
forest marked by last year's epic
flood level.

2.

Cautious deer lie curled near the earthen
divide's windbreak while a spotted eagle
    lands on a red elm
standing alone in a ditch. Like them,
I patiently await the morning sun's grace.
    Then, as I downshift
the Honda over patches of black ice,
my thoughts divert from the urologic
    Destiny, the U of I
hospitals. "Ke me tto" I beseech
the winged Grandfather. "From a place
    where high water
and age once displaced many from
presumption or sheer experience,
    protect my family.
Because we tend to persist. Else why
would Selene and I stay home in

the middle
of a flood twenty-eight years ago?

3.

Which may be the reason I always
dream Selene and I are caught in a debris-
        cluttered flood,
with a large wave crashing toward us,
snapping young new trees alongside
        an unseen road.
While the event is blatantly surreal, its
portrayal of our demise is nonetheless
        an all-encompassing
ordeal.

4.

Today there's no equivalent. But
Eventuality, in a failed mode, surfaces
        through the smoky
whispers of would-be conspirators
discussing another coup. No, I answer
        without being
asked. Christ no, I lost an Angel
the last time. Literally. In spite of non-
        ordinary
indications, I related from inside
their tarp-covered hut, more than
        maple saplings
fell during the tribal and gaming
operations takeover. For instance,
        the night
before the casino was closed
by federal court order, a hallway
        at home issued
voices in English. And when we
approached, they vanished into
        the whipping
curtains of the kids' bedroom
window. Maybe authorities

at 12:01 a.m.
unsealing the envelope?
we later questioned.

5.

Society Wolverine looks for approval,
advises Selene. But you're not there—
    right? Because
the moonlit guard followed you from
Whisky Bottom Road. And when it ruffled
    its back and bared
its tusks, you reached out cautiously
over the meadow. That's when a plane
    ripped apart in
mid-night, showering the Settlement
with silver shards. That wasn't rain.
    And when your
son envisions a Wolverine mask
on your face, it's a contradiction
    that'll require
cleansing with smoke, especially
the kind that's passed through
    a spearhead
embedded with tiny, fossilized
seashells lest you be exhumed
    biting your hand—
a symbol of failed resistance.

KAMDEN QUADRANGLE

1

.

The Black Eagle Child Settlement,
at daybreak, serves as a conduit
  for the boy
psychics who are known locally
as Two Brothers or *We si me ti a ki.*
  When "1333
Appomattox" is announced as being
the potential whereabouts, the moon's
  pallid memory
turned green over the melting
frost-covered lawn. Here, before
  the address
was jotted down, Edgar dreamt
his heart underwent a Bud Light
  transfusion.
As lava sculpted his arthritic
veins, a Mountain Ram
  was visually
conjured, which was being
agitated by a three-legged dog
  the boys
named Ours.

2.

When the dirt cliffs broke, bright
tan chunks landed near the standoff
  where Edgar
held his son, Listening Bear, tightly.
Then, he zoomed the telephoto lens
  on the Ram's
hooves clacking over the purple
railroad track rocks. For safety
  he ran to a house,
the one that isn't there anymore.
This includes the adjacent earth lodge

and its name-giving
songs. With his son still in his arms,
Ours slammed against the doorway.
            And a moment
before the blessing of place
and numbers, Selene related
            a Wolverine
in her sleep was being chased
away from a childhood yard
            by a loud Black
Duck.

3.

So before Kamden Quadrangle stirs
to the Euro-staccato of Saturday
            morning
profanity and TV cartoons, a pot
of water was already "stove-
            standing."
And then a map off the Internet
was re-examined twice. Before the boys'
oatmeal cooled, an ocean-submerged
Boar in its role as savior was also
            described:
With obsidian teeth tied as arrow tips,
"Andrew Caleb" practice-aims
            a long bow
at a picnic bench. Those present
by speakerphone learn he's lonely
            for blue
conical shells appearing
beneath the sand-speckled
            froth.

4.

Further, as the boys' backpacks
were being adjusted by Selene,
            they reflected
that Andrew seeks sun-warmed

flesh. For its sacredness. But
        the words
whispered into a walkie-talkie
puzzled them: "A coast-to-coast
        impalement."
As Edgar attempted to explain
what the archer-pig's words
        could mean,
the older boy related a hand
from the bench signaled
        an OK,
"like this." The after-trail
of his small but quick hand
        left an imprint
in our minds of a dark needle
spiraling out from the orange
        serrated clouds,
symbolizing impermanence
perhaps for someone by
        9 AM EST.

THE LONE SWIMMER OF HENRY COUNTY, VIRGINIA

ESP? We're not discounting anything at this stage.
—Undersheriff Earl Tassel, The Roanoke Messenger

Undersheriff: On a belated experimental basis,
after missing persons investigations have stalled,
like the Anna Goodchild case of Vallejo, California,
or the high school cheerleaders' dual internment
in acrylic in Washington state, I reluctantly
proffer my observations to authorities. Typically,
from the four images, several factors will coincide
with the crime scene evidence. Some departments reply,
while others, I believe, simply take. So investigations,
like American poetry, if I may opine, can become
political for clairvoyants and poets alike. While
Western civilization pegs Native Americans
as superstitious, there's nevertheless an illustrious
history of ESP. Ironically, in Black Eagle Child
Society, any claim "to see things" that others can't
is considered inapplicable because this practice
was apparently misplaced as a gift. However,
Shamanism, to use a quirky noun, isn't earned
through religious teachings per se; it simply
dwells in the psyche until harnessed with
revelations, depending on one's receptivity.
With nay adieu, the lead vehicle, at least for
me, is a Lazy Boy recliner. Regarding Juniper
Court and her murdered grandparents, enclosed
are thoughts the chair provided on her whereabouts.
But first, there's torment because her uncle who
reportedly failed to take this eight-year-old girl
fishing is like me. Often too self-centered
perhaps, a child's wish is neglected:

Monday, August 26th, 2002

After touching an Internet-posted photograph
of Juniper on the computer monitor, I sit

blindfolded in the basement filled with cedar smoke.
The chair cradles me, rocking me as Grandmother
once did. Supported with prayer, the sacred tobacco
has been placed beside a tree for guidance.
The notepad meets my pencil in the cool darkness.
As the first impressions collect I gradually discern:

1. An old-time telephone with separate
 mouth and ear pieces that also transposes
as an old phonograph, a record player,
the kind with a cone-shaped speaker minus
the listening-dog logo. This dualistic apparatus
exudes a vortex force capable of attracting human
and nonhuman substance, going beyond
RCA purpose.

2. Glock model pistol, caliber unknown.

3. A bemused chicken, literally, with
a high-powered telescope, either about
to look into a viewfinder or withdrawing
after a view.

4. The name Clifford Murdoch
or Murdock, followed by 4311 and then EXY.

Tuesday, August 27th

5. Initially, a lone woman submerged
in semi-translucent water, stationary at
first, and then she's diving at an eight
o'clock angle into a river's stone-walled
and bubbling depth. Wearing a light colored
rubber cap with an early '50s one-piece
swimsuit, the woman's body propels
itself like a torpedo.

6. A woman swimmer reappears, only
this time she's on the surface, swimming
rapidly. She soon dissolves and is replaced
with a cartoon-like rabbit whose face and ears

are stretched back and distorted due,
apparently, to high rate of speed.

Wednesday, August 28th

9. An image of a shower-in-progress, by itself.
Then view pans to shower drain holes. Before
a tangent of an aircraft intercedes, a question
arises: could a bullet shell casing squeeze
through the drain?

10. A baseball batter in a nearly completed
swing reminds me of an old trading card
that's been color-enhanced. Later, the number
22 is seen on the posed batter's short-
brimmed cap.

11. A shiny helicopter propeller in motion.

12. A sitting person who is unable to
walk, but it's unclear if individual is female
or male and even what age.
Note: That night I dreamt of lily white hands
held as if in Christian prayer. Like
a sculpture, they're crafted from soft fabric.
Are there landmarks of such in vicinity? Also,
I should mention a Glock pistol can be fitted
with a .22 caliber barrel; and the chicken,
as a voyeur, could've made an obscene
telephone call to the Courts as the media
reported, qualifying to an extent
the non-ordinary RCA speaker.

Thursday, August 29th

13. An oversized gorilla holding a female
who's attired in a white dress with loud red
flowers. Said creature dips her delicately
into the religious water, with the focus
shifting to his cupped hands.

14. *Walford.*

15. *1606 Walford Avenue.*

Saturday, October 5th synopsis—after the discovery
of Juniper's remains in Booneville, North Carolina.
When I faxed the first images with numbers to your
office and after haphazard cartographic research,
I thought a body was wedged in the Hillpott Reservoir
turbines or in the tunnels under Martinsdale. In retrospect,
had I Internet-searched "4311" for North Carolina instead
of Virginia, Highway 311 might have emerged, which
was 411 historically. This is the road that passes
through Lockingham County, near where she
was found and close to the prehistoric rock-lined
fish dams. Of the female swimmer—could this
be the famous college swimmer known simply
as Princess? Is she still alive? And "EXY"
backward signifies the Saskatoon Airport.
This is the direction a suspect allegedly
fled on his way to the Yukon Territory. Right?
And "1606" may pertain to early American
settlers. This area resonates with impassioned
secrecy. Sadly, there are times when I, too, as
actress Annette Benning once script-recited,
"need an interpreter." It's interesting how
my children are unusually vociferous today
about fishing. They're banging gear upstairs,
while their mother is making a shore lunch
of peanut butter and jelly sandwiches
and Kool-Aid. Into a small plastic jar
I carefully pour sacred tobacco which
the Underwater Deities will receive from
each child before the bait is cast. Sir, from
the hinterlands and in Juniper's memory,
I politely take leave for an overdue parental
obligation. If this case is ever solved in our
lifetimes, could you please let me
and the Lazy Boy know? Signed—
Edgar Bearchild.

NI TANATOTA-MA NI-E YE-ME KWI TE E YA NI, I WILL TALK ABOUT THIS WHILE I STILL REMEMBER

1.

And on this hilltop, in elaborate
ancient villages, is where we converged
for the Primitive Guests Show. Twice daily,
a quarter mile strip through the World's Fair
was cordoned off for Act One. When loud-
speakers announced us as "people born
with acute senses, the kind needed to
survive a wilde existenst," we marched
to the Hell-on-Scorn River. Also marking
the hour were trumpets wailing from distant
castle towers that were mounted with anti-
aircraft guns aimed at the mountainous
horizon. While "their womenfolk"
pretended to fill clay jars, we languidly
stood guard in the foliage. No one knew
what "acute" meant, but the river
affected our breathing. Although our
invite seemed like an apology albeit
disguised from Mineral King heirs,
a century made no difference.

2.

The earth's decay tumbled in our veins
as minute pieces of glass. And we each
lived "the depravity," not vicariously as
was once perceived. When it crystallized
in our lungs, we were reminded in our x-rays
of a half-lion, half-serpent creature, holding
a metal shield and sword. He's still looking
in those caves, the elders forewarned, with
its tail hooked to a glowing lantern.

371

3.

When the Fair's music was turned off,
we'd escort the women back from
the shoreline. Later, with wild-eyed
passengers screaming from Ferris Wheel
carriages outside our windows, we'd
prepare for Act 2. With the sides of our
shaved heads decorated with ochre paint,
we'd kneel in the circus tent's shade,
tapping out high-energy rhythms
on the iron stakes with our bows.
While long-legged grotesque clowns
bantered with crowds from behind
the ropes, a speckled dove's cry
signaled an arrowless assault
of a giant billboard depicting
a 3-D stampede of bison. Named
"Wilde Beeste," it huffed like an
old train, *ke ta - we sko te wi.* Mostly
I recall the fire truck crews who
doubled as the King's security,
dousing flames that started from
one out-of-control beeste.

4.

And directly below the villages,
in buildings that resemble horse
stalls, is where we slept. We were
billed as "living museum displays."
Once, from under a bright yellow
umbrella, a bourgeoisie lady sighed:
"Isn't Act 3 pathetically adorable?"
In agreement, the partygoers tipped
their cups of clear dandelion wine.
Culturally, we were misrepresented.
And with fair-goers drawn instead
to the dada-like sculptures at
the Pavilion of History, it didn't

matter. Either way, we made fifty
krekoz a day. Plus, we could take
an extra boiled egg for breakfast
or refill our wine bags at supper.

5.

Carved from marbled iridescent
cheese, the sculpture-oddities were
called "Homage to an Indigenous Past."
Life-sized, they stood in refrigerated
rooms. With our forebears depicted
as having green eyes that glowed at night,
leaping from tree to tree, we danced by
in our jingling, painted moccasins.
By nightfall, like the other Guests,
we stretched out our meal with
gayety. And when we got "mizzed"
to the point that ballads of unknown
languages sounded familiar, ghosts
woke us up, reminding us of Bruce's
song that we were born in the USA . . .

6.

And way over there, toward the left
by the trees, is the Hallway of Dioramas.
It's a tent-like building where we were
once mistaken for Gray Wolves. At
gunpoint, plainclothes agents frisked us
for flint-tipped terror. Afterwards, we
dance-posed beside realistic-looking
animals, our namesake, most of whom
died in the Great Drought. All summer,
inside the Pillar of World Foods, we ate
supper under a giant fresco of military
Earthquake tanks. Beneath their wheels,
hands with white flags waved from
the trenches.

7.

On days petro and rations were
distributed, Salvettoreo, the village
muralist did sketches presumably
for future wars. But the weekly pay,
Dear God, *zaah,* that's how much
was made a year previous for
10,000 pages of tribal myths.
As "highly skilled archers," we
were there at the Mineral King
heirs behest, yes, but we were
also featured in a monolithic
stone theatre where robotic
lions savagely dismembered
mannequins. We did Act 4
without complaint. Because
what mattered most was for
our beloved grandparents,
oceans away, to eat well.
*"So who's the ungrateful
heathen now?"* we mockingly
sang to the three little pigs
in our declaratory songs
of war after wiring
shoonya to the Why
Cheer National
Bank.

FOR LADY Z BEFORE SHE BECAME A TERRORIST

1.

    Soon, barely holding on, the ice-glazed
branch of the birch tree will snap in the quick
                October breeze,
releasing a yellow-green leaf to the edge
of the campus sidewalk. There,
    largely unnoticed,
it'll deteriorate under a blanket of new
snow. Quietly. We're no different,
           with each
shadow destined for Grandmother's
ceremony where large fields
    of swaying grass
await themselves to change into
cures, a defense against wandering
                protoplasmic
diseases, *a be ne we ni.*

2.

    In increments the earth readjusts
herself, affecting our daily gauntlet
    of emotions from afar.
Whatever we experience, that's taken
and grinded between rocks into a powdery
            form of serenity.
And thereafter, like a small pool of fresh
rainwater that trembles imperceptibly
    to the dark,
shifting ground beneath, its pulse,
depth, and alchemy is closer than
           a digested
turtle's heart. Even when its tender
life is removed from its body

and shell,
there's a profound
change.

3.

It is therefore said in myth
or in life, there's deceit and betrayal.
          For that
aberration, there's no reason nor
palpable defense. Even among relatives
                              or friends,
vulnerability is a light jacket
against a hailstorm. Like the time
          we detected
her presence by clasping
our father's hand, the one crippled
                    by fifty
years of "word-collecting."
The next day, the serenity we
          had sprinkled
over the meadow's rainwater
floated as dry clumps beside
                              the wary
motionless bugs.

4.

Verily, as she had once
confided by email, the Kyle Photo
          meeting
was coincidence. During a quest
for a missing boy of Santa Fe,
                    New Mexico,
other things that should've been
detected weren't. What father
          didn't know
was the side that eventually
resonated on the hospital

                              television
as a passport snapshot.
On the faraway mountaintops,
            near the village
where she lived, blue-tinted snow
made the sky over the valley calm,
                              brilliant,
and intriguingly portentous.

5.

    Eventually, Lady Z, computer
engineer, this weather will descend
            into this familiar
landscape. There, if only to remind
visitors or even newcomers, black
                         and white
animal deities will also reconstruct
messages on the opaque floor.
    Soon, before
changing into the shiny back
of a sea-faring creature, the floor
                         is decorated
with pencil strokes, signifying
the genesis of letters. Are we,
        therefore,
amenable to seeing ourselves
as descendants from this
                         theoretical
marriage that was made through
a bridge of cold crystal?

6.

    As snowflakes land on our jackets,
we dream-hear the flute or *ne ne kwa*
            being played
by Grandmother whose gracious hat
made of high billowing clouds envelops

us as a shadow.
Her presence transports our thoughts
to one another. And before Fire
        snuffs out
numbers appearing as 8-8-8
in braided serpents, the missing boy
                is tossed
by his captors into an abandoned mine
near Zerrillos Park. When the train's
        whistle echoes
a mile away, causing paralysis
in my sleep, had the ropes on
                        the boy
already tightened from
the useless struggle?

SOMEWHERE, NEW MEXICO

The
fish-faced
caterpillar,
the one
we photo-
graphed on
the trampoline this
summer—all radiant with
its green, yellow, and black skin colors, has entombed
itself in a place called Zerrillos Regional Park. Driving parallel
with the railroad tracks, Bob,
my professor emeritus
observer and his pet, Rio,
hydroplane Waldo Road
in a diabolical truck. To
the north, the black volcanic
escarpment and to the south
arroyos. From the pale east
the search party and to
the west the potential
of their discovery.
Four days previous.
I described jade-speckled flood
water flowing into a hollow edifice. A shimmering,

watery-   shaped hand   changed
into a   bear paw,   surfacing like
a submarine.   Soon, *das*   *boot* bellied-up
                      and long
                      amber claws
                      in glowing
                      patina
                      became
                      spouts
                      situated
                      over a

                    whirlpool.
                       In oblique
                       contact
                       with
                       the
                     Swan
                   Epi-
                   phany,
                 Selene
                   drew
                       a lizard's
                       torso
                       perched
                       on
                       a

                    black sphere.
              Like us, it was transfixed
             by the gurgling, re-channeled
            water. The Romano search party is
            close, but we're omnipresent. And Bob
          captures the jagged rocks, blessing grass,
        pinon, and juniper on film. Annabeth, Anna-
        beth, he must be thinking, which script are
            you studying now? Did the director of
            WHAT THE FREAK call your agent?
And would you consider the role of Brook Grassleggings? Bearchild asks. Sign a
photo for him on your next visit; he named a daughter after you. He's also the reason
I'm here with Rio, drifting sideways over long abandoned mines in a pickup. Like
a dormant metal detector that becomes animated, Rio is affected by surreal hues of
light emanating from the open coliseum windows in the distance. High above, long
gray sheets of rain descend from a thundercloud, covering the valley. Whatever proof
that may have been there becomes an echo amid the periodic wailing of trains. Verily,
this is a place where Mountain lions avoid humanity by draping their shadows over
prickly pear and cholla, a place where the scent of corn being ground into meal on a
metate no longer drifts over their lightning-lit trails.

THE THREE BROTHERS, 1999

1.

Sir, with a fourth murder reported
at Yosemite, I'm re-submitting
"Long Distance Observations"
to your Sacramento regional office.
    Enclosed also
are copies of my college faculty
and tribal enrollment cards. As
noted before, I was once asked
to work on a missing person case.
        It was informal,
to say the least: I was guest speaker
at a justice department lunch when
a spouse of a drug and firearms
official brought the subject up.
        Later, over
cookies and coffee, I affirmed
my interest with tribal-based
intuition. While *questing* for
victims or their captors
        probably
began as disguised grief—
in having been indirectly
affected, this experiment
was then reinforced by an
        unprompted
dream. Its images were
shared with your office,
including references who
should attest I live near
        the Why Cheer
and Gladwood townships
in central Iowa.

2.

Here, we believe some people
can see what others can't.
Culturally and conceivably
applicable, our word is:
       Ne a bi a ki.
While such gifts of healing
and seeing were probably
misplaced ages ago, an
exception took place,
       I believe,
in 1999. If only for a few
days. But everything had
started before via a friend's
suspicious death. Traveling
       beyond
speculation was unplanned.
Yes, Bertie C. of Texarkana
gave us the suspects' clan
name ties, the apparel worn
       that night,
and the forensics therein.
She knew two had fled to
Nebraska, making closure
elusive. Here, convincing
       authorities
was preceded by a history
of mistreatment of Indians.
Inevitably, time corroborated
outcome. Bertie said when
       suspects
became shells of their
former selves, death by
alcohol would glisten on
their faces, and a prison cell
       would have
no witnesses when cardiac
arrest occurs. Then, years
later and after a four-day fast,
when my wife touched my
       dehydrated,

but emotionally-sensitive
body, I thought I knew things.
            Briefly.

3.

When the Lazy Boy recliner
helps, numbers and letters
appear under a Dutch bandana
blindfold. Some take the shape
            of hovering
fireflies who paint scenes
of faraway places. These geo-
markers are then checked on
the Internet. For Yosemite,
            however,
an invisible portal extended
from the living room window
like a hallway over the gravel
driveway. Thus, on the first
            three victims,
tribal homeland life became
distended one March afternoon.
Following a meal of fried
potatoes and onions, Walleye
            fillets,
with cold Rolling Rock beer,
I fell asleep. With post-lecture
thoughts on Blackfeet myths
receding as bluish-grey swirls
            of smoke,
the chair became my late
grandmother's soft arms.
After being placated, I dreamt
I had walked through the picture
            window,
stepping out cautiously into
an opaque hallway.

4.

Suspended in mid-air over the gravel
driveway, the TV news report on
the missing sightseers re-appeared.
As the academic day dissolved,
   the persona
of the missing mother who was
in the car with two girls enveloped
me. In need of directions, words were
exchanged with two dark, haggard-
   looking men.
In a spark of consciousness,
however, the license plate
number of the Nissan Sentra
the men got out of was lost.

5.

So, on April 28, mostly from guilt,
I initiated a session with the Lazy-
Boy. Four numbers were conjured,
including an image of a billboard
   of a tilted
bottle with its contents of water
splashing. These numbers are what
to Yosemite? I asked Alta Vista.
Bed and breakfast place at 7110
   Ledgeway Inn,
it answered as option. With bottle
symbol, I read the Melosso family,
from one of the young victims,
owned a small bottling business
   in Uruguay.

6.

On the third visitation, there
were three barely-visible bodies.
They were laying down and floating

inches above an unseen ground.
                    Before
the theatrical-like shapes
became transparent, a single tire-
width band rolled in and went over
each of these motionless torsos,
                    tracing
curves with vivid yellow paint.
On the paper nearby I wrote:
"Three hills? Three peaks?"
Further inquiry brought
        a Ruger
.22 caliber pistol, followed by
"LS 2250." A Chevy Silverado
truck, answered Alta Vista. As
for "Three peaks," a pervasive
                    Landmark
called the Three Brothers
surfaced.

7.

Imparted while en route to
the college, the fourth revelation
wasn't encouraging. Uninvited,
a luminescent picture self-
                    assembled
itself on the windshield. From
the shadowy fields zipping by,
I soon took notice of the shape
of two people. They were in
        a car trunk
in fetal positions. Abruptly,
the mother sat up and gestured
with her middle finger. My wife,
Selene Buffalo Husband, consoled
        it was probably
intended for the culprit, not
the beholder. This was reassuring.
Unlike seers who relive lethal attacks—
all but assuming a victim's demise,

385

mine dealt
with names, numbers, and geo-
markers. But whenever that failed,
overt things happened, like physical
contact with cool drops of water
                    landing or forks
levitating for attention. It can also
be complicated. Like some ghost
asking a personal question for which
there isn't any self-empowering
                    answer to serve
as a bridge toward Intangibility.
Do you find me attractive?

8.

Next, when Selene related three
Iowans were missing in Colorado
and that psychics may have been
contacted by family members,
        I mistakenly
thought Yosemite was the topic.
So when Alta Vista pointed to
The Gold Pick newspaper,
a photograph was revealed:
                    of the mother
and daughter sitting beside
the Merced River. Was it taken
by the Melosso girl? I wondered.
*A photograph speaks time-jumping
                    language,*
I later wrote, *like the Three Brothers
jutting skyward as mountains.* In
a band of loud yellow paint, they had
outlined the three sightseers' torsos.
        Not expecting
a formal reply, I asked you: Sir,
are the peaks the same ones
the Lazy-Boy illustrated?

9.

On July 9, from under a bandana,
I whispered a prayer in Black Eagle
Child, hoping for the elusive license plate.
When three revolving letters were
        provided,
they originally appeared in faint neon
as "EAM." Then they reversed places
briefly like a fancy marquee display.
When this happened, the name
        "Ed"
strobe light-flashed. Next came
an image of a lone peyote rattle
beside an old skeletal man. From
this layout, a ferocious snake,
        baring fangs
wrote number "11." With
the snake punched sideways,
the numbers became "77."

10.

On July 10, an elongated goose neck
image added an "S" to the numerical
snake. Thus "S 11 77" transposed
to "VS 11 77" or was it "V5 11 77?"
        Then, when
I adduced the feathered deity's
neck held up the four earth lodge
poles, the rugged race of the first
person who had approached
        the Zunde
vehicle appeared. He leaned down
to the window. There was a "skin
opening" and "Diego." The last
manifestation was a scaffold
        made of four
bright wrenches holding up
two other wrenches.

11.

That imparted, had it not been
for the fourth murder of another
female, which happened close
to said bed and breakfast inn,
              I may not
have written. From the Hinterlands,
I resolve to live with the fact that
the three revolving letters, EAM,
which were previously sent by fax,
              are part
of the current suspect's vehicle
license plate. Further, as noted before,
the four numbers 2469 via my home
telephone are the same as license plate—
        only they
flank the EAM in reverse. At first,
I was reluctant to accept this last
coincidence. Mostly, I thought
I'd be wrong in believing that
              anyone
would concur these apparitions
were right.

DRIFTWOOD OVER MY HEART

For the now ill-fated
tribal business committee meeting,
the one that caused years of compound financial debt,
if not ruin, Bearchild testified in his own defense,
"I wore Samurai-type
armor that day, your
Honors, symbolically-
speaking." Underneath
his Salmon pink-colored
shirt were two intersecting
bandoliers of counter-
attacking medicines.
"Namely, the dark purple seeds
of the white spear-shaped clusterberry
leaves."   Designed to repel sorcery, they were
placed over his   torso at daybreak.   "For what purpose?"
sked Tribe's   ear-ringed   and bemused lawyer.
To keep   madnesse and   other intrusions—maybe
ke you, away."   Later, during last   comments,   Bearchild
urther delineated the bandoliers' use. "Numbering eight, the small
eather bundles are tied with shiny green strips of new cloth that
orms, in effect, a permeable but unseen barrier." Acting
letached, the lawyer named Thor swung his obscene pony tail as he faced the peace
ribunal. Baring teeth profusely dotted with bits of black banana, he faked a grin and
mplored, "Come on, Ed, we discussed this before lunch." Bearchild replied that no

ry bread was broken, that food was sacred and not intended for lawyers nor lobbyists. On
oan for a thousand years, Bearchild explained the bandoliers' contents came from a
enevolent spirit of a water fowl. To those entrusted to carry it, the harvested charm could
hwart ill-will. But it couldn't change the vote of the business committee to invest in what

e argued would be less than minimal returns from high profile lobbyists. "To activate the
lriftwood, the carrier's voice is required," he told the Honors. To which one reacted by
urling his silver eyebrows into a mobile albino caterpillar, while another coiled one
eather-wrapped braid to his thumb. But the one in the middle looked aloof and sedated.

389

"Even if I was just clearing my raspy throat or feigning a cough, like I did when I enter
this room, a wall of debris from a flood will swirl invisibly. No one can cross it to
dissuade one's convictions. And if an attempt is made, it's deflected." When dissensio
morphed into grown men standing around him, defending progeny wrought by marital
   infidelity or the prospect therein, his elderly parents hiked to the Goddesses
Spring and harvested roots that resembled driftwood. There, high atop the secluded
hillside that was enshrouded by fog that's lit up by the sun's orange haze, deity names
   were invoked one-by-one. The roots solidified and became bitter to the taste.
Seeing himself as an   ancient Asian warrior,   wielding a sword,   he could hear the
armor rattling   like a   Supernatural   roused from   its underground lair. In self-
       defense mode,   it began scanning   the chambers floor, rotating left,
                         purifying, then right,
                         nullifying disorder.
                         Next, the reed
                            interwoven
                            breast plate
                            morphed from
                            a Gatling gun
                            to a desert ally.
                         As either presence
                         would know, as either
                         could ostensibly discern:

Ma ni ke-ma tti-na at wi no ni. This is bad medicine (witchcraft). Lethal daggers carve

from	prehistoric	bones tested	my anti-hoodoo.	Affixed	under my love
Gatsby	shirt,	a telephone	set to silent	awaits	a call
from	Daisy	of East	Quail	Road,	Why Cheer,

5	2	3	3	9

THE LAST DAY GEESE DRONES CIRCLED HOME

A small midnight, the one that
was previously thought uneventful,
          has left
a self-portrait entitled *"December,*
next to a set of gray insipid eyes."
          Minus
a signature, this etching sits on a desk,
glowing a faint neon green from a frame
          that's
varnished and inlaid with thin slices
of walnut shells. In their skeletal
          intricacy,
the shells glisten, flashing
intermittently. And shortly before
          daybreak,
when the blanket-door is unfastened,
I am transported skyward by my
          outstretched
arms, with the fingertips acting
as the jet propulsion source.

As a straw-filled cadaver on
a nonessential horse, my spine
          is tied
onto a saddle with thick sinew
and propped up with v-shaped
          saplings,
the ones that were harvested beside
a glacier-fed stream. Eviscerated
          and therefore
alone, I lurch nosily into a moonlit
camp of kind, unsuspecting relatives.
          In this
near-catatonic moment, as beads
on my quirt dimly reflect stars,
          I recall
parts of an old dream regarding

a crimson-tinted Buddha figurine.
        Belatedly,
I wonder whether it's actually
buried *a ka me e ki,* across
            the river
in a soybean field as previously
indicated.

Should I have heeded the Black
Coyote's sign then, I mentally
                type,
instead of finding solace in
a campus town knick-knack
            purchase?
It's evident my morning-singing
relatives will see me for what I've
        always been:
an imperfect, frugal messenger
whose parfleche holds so little
        of anything.
But the greater question flickering
behind the Self Worth Pool Hall
                sign is this:
to whom or to what am I an after-
trail? That of history itself or
            per chance
a fiery, indomitable star?

By visual projection I'm relegated,
not appointed, to wander the unholy
        prairies
of aluminum where I'll speechlessly
implore all parties met or detected:
            are you
translating everything I say onto
a loom again? Including how a once-
                extinct
mountain lion genetically willed
itself to its present form? *Zaah,*
        that's
a conflagration of secrecy,

so to speak. Here, I'd appeal to any
        cosmic
tribunal that Fate in the guise
of weather will extinguish hinterland
            practices.
Especially when they exceed science
and morph to harmful presumptions.
            Like now.

Framed supernaturally, please
know the delicate combustibility
            of nature:
that if you discover above-referenced
predator's tracks circling back to
                its half-eaten
prey in your backyard, it will not
budge from its time-jumping path.
            Because it
was there when survival maps
known as Third Earth Scrolls
        were first
distributed by the Deities.

Moreover, on the day Tribe
deployed two geese drones over
            the Black
Eagle Child Settlement, symbolizing
a pair's journey to the Grandfather
                World,
we were confused about which color
best addresses our collective grief.
            And we
asked which color denotes the fact
they were taken for unknown reasons.
        After witnessing
Luciano ingest eight spoonfuls
of memories related to tracer fire
            in the Valley
of Reluctance, we surrendered.
And we admitted this inequity
                of experience

exists. In resolve we lift our arthritic
arms to the window and wave from
              a place soon
scheduled for decoration with
the apocalyptic plumes of frost.

THE ROCK'S MESSAGE

My
grand-
son
is a
snapping
turtle   who first came   to me
as a gray rock, a sign
surfacing from our yard on
a hill. Over several weeks, I
began digging around the sides
with my walking stick. Slowly it took
shape as this benign visitor. Whereas
his father is fourteen, school means I
assume care duties. In the breeze
I sense the apple tree's shade
emanating a sweet and cool
taste. On my bruises the
leaves   seem to say: you   are ok.
Yes,
you
are
ok.
Ok?

ULTRASOUND, THE MISSING PLANE, DOWN UNDER

In the technician's bony but supple
hands a body-seeing instrument charts
    the oceanic
topography of my syrup-laden torso.
After being jostled about, my kidney
        winces as it
minutely assembles its sponge-like
shape through the kinetic sounds
        of valleys
and mountains being strewn
across the vast floor by an eagle's
        wing.

Then, before supper and while
discussing the missing, it makes
    a clairvoyant
projection: "Willy-Willy Gulch."
A pensive teenager, the one named
        Listening
Bear who's also our son and who's
said to see what others can't,
        pays special
attention as a description is proffered:
"It's a place along the west coast
        where divine
winds originate. And I fear that's
the only clue."

Later, however, under the influence
of a smothered burrito, the kidney
    confides
per direction of red dust storms is
where airliner might be located.
        Notes and quick
sips of cold beer are taken as
a song "Helena Beat" plays on TV
        in the next

room. Silhouetted by the screen's
flashing light, the loquacious
        kidney,
with fork and coffee in hand,
surmises the prehistoric tangent
   is Kalgoorlie,
a subterranean connection
where echoes from a chasm
      near Perth
have taken searchers
too far out.

With the medical scope retracted,
the visitor politely takes leave
          of the table,
leaving us like untouched plates
on intricately-woven reed mats.
    And before
we knew it had started,
the hinterland rite was done.
   Only in
dreams thereafter would we
recall how this presence
      remained
stationary in the current
by oscillating its bright yellow
       fins.
Thus, from a faraway place
where memories and inverted
     stars whir
assuredly beneath the coral
reef, we are overwhelmed,
   if not
transfixed, by the water's
primordial sanctity.

A LIFE-SHAPING SPOON

The clear, plastic spoon, which *Ketikona*,
Eagle Feather, keeps in a school backpack,
is a tangible indicator of change. In this case,
it's the all-important name of a newlywed
kindergarten teacher. With a summer-
reddened face, Amy arrives and soon
becomes a Mrs., making the spoon
a keepsake. Since it came from
a draped table of a glorious party
where a giant cake was served,
it's arguably a life-shaping utensil,
the kind you can see through
and examine under safety. And
it's insignificant if he wasn't there
or whether the spoon was used
for a mid-morning snack. What
matters is what it means to Amy—
and ostensibly for him. So we clean
it in the kitchen sink with diligence
and add it to his basket of sunlit
possessions.

SHE SAID I KNOW MORE THAN YOUR KIDS AND GRANDKIDS

On that windy day our words at first were traveling
peacefully on spider webs. There was no war
      to speak of
because it had ended eons ago. That's when
everyone concurred with what they were,
      or rather who
they were designated to be. Whether
it was a rock, fire, water, tree, animal,
      bird, river,
star, sun, moon, and so forth. Each
had a role to oversee and, if necessary,
      make changes
on The Second Earth. And so it
was unsettling how the day's events
      evolved from
incinerating "wooden jelly fish"
(as we jokingly called clumps
      of black
dirt clinging to roots of young trees)
to witnessing womanly-voiced spirits
      create
micro-bursts of emotion and energy
on the hillside. In re-living the vast
      incongruities
of dreams, passive one-cloud
rains, and spade shovels that started
      the land
clearing, womanly stars, for no
apparent reason, lapsed into bouts
      of
unrelenting sadness.

THE LONELY CRICKETS THEATRE

To the maker of the sapling
    dwelling
that sits low and therefore
undetected in the green sunlit
    clearing
of the thickets nearby, lonely
crickets have gathered to watch
a small geodesic dome-shaped
    lodge,
ttaki-abagaikani, unravel its bindings.
Using shards of daylight and long
grass to tie the bent branches together,
you sculpt a running fox that soon
    transforms
into a series of creatures thought
long extinct. As a young, unknowing
child, I stand still as they are delicately
resurrected one by one—the saber
tooth lion, the woolly mammoth,
    and the others—
from the rock under the dark layered
soil of woodlands and prairie histories.
According to crickets, especially
Crestwood School of Social
Research alumni, the glaciers
stopped here and retreated.
    This
precious clearing, they elucidate,
is therefore the past, a testament in
the present world that memory
is a reflection of all Afterlife,
that everything is déjà vu
in Grandfather's eternal
metro cinema, that all
    things
eventually return.

FOR YOU, A HANDFUL OF THE GREATEST GIFT

Small-eyed, plump, and with black
leathery hands, *Attaskwa,* is composed
        and debonair
as it perches on trampled cat tail reeds
beside a quivering, cloud-reflecting pond.
        "Filled
with cosmogony, he's exceedingly
unselfish," instructs the branch-shaping
        sculptor.
"*Wabami*, Look at him, *kekenetama,*
he knows. And he's elated to oversee
        what
the daylight brings everyday."
We focus the camera's telephoto lens
        and see
details of his coat glittering with drops
of luminescent water.

"To our Grandfather, *Kemettoemenana,*"
narrates the sculpture, "he magnanimously
        agreed after
the Last Conflict of the Gods to retrieve
a handful of soil from the deep, singular
        ocean that
became land beneath our feet. He
set forth unequivocally a doctrine.
        Listen
very closely, my grandchildren,
nottisemetike, for you may not hear
        these words
again." Lifting its black nose
to the sky, *Attaskwa* ambles
        to the pond's
edge and stops as if to pose
before the picture is snapped.
        Behind us,
the sculptor crafts a small

dome-shaped skeletal lodge
        and
embeds it to the ground.

We wholly agree that each day
there are overt and minute changes.
        Even if we
don't see or if we're not there, it happens.
Without Muskrat, our Creation—you
        and me,
would be zero. From the alluvial soil
delivered from oceanic depths, we
        were made
thereafter. His courage is brazen like
that of a *Wetase,* Veteran, because he
        dove
unflinchingly to retrieve Earth.

Oblivious of our presence, *Attaskwa*
slides into the pond and swims
        to the middle,
creating a cape-like effect of waves
behind him that dissipates
        the blue sky
and its clouds. Indicative of his
sacrifice, we learn *Attaskwa* floated
        lifeless
to the surface. In gratitude Earth-maker
resurrected him. So when personal
        contributions
are contemplated, ask yourself,
my daughter and son, what did I
        sacrifice?
Think specifically of what he did.
Use him, my children, *netabenoemetike,*
        as an example
of what must be done to rectify
society's misdirection. Only then
        will our,
language, religion, culture, and history
thrive in the Muskrat's benevolent
        shadow.

As he approaches the mound
of his home, *Attaskwa* looks back
          at us briefly.
And before his cape of waves reaches
the shoreline, he dives into the dark
          green pond.
Before we pack up the equipment,
the sculptor hands us sacred
          tobacco
to sprinkle delicately over
the water animal's architectural
          tranquility.

FOOTPRINTS MADE OF SNOW

As a squadron of vintage
British military airplane
    drones
in camouflage preceded us
over the runaway, which
    was
just a half-frozen cornfield
near the Rolling Puffball
    neighborhood,
I already knew the first
falling snow of November
    would
recite *e tti so wa ni* my name
and follow me seemingly
    on
the way home, filling
my jagged tracks
    each
time they imprinted
the soft, earth-rumbling
    mud.

GATE 632

I

"Maximus radius or vice versa"
are words saber-flashing in my sleep.
        Eventually,
at daybreak, amid a long train
of randomly-issued phrases—
first in English and then Black Eagle
Child, a Great Lakes Algonquin dialect,
        I awaken
and find myself holding an old blood-
letting horn to my ear. Absent,
        however, is my
grandmother's exposed back
with the long razor's nicks that leaves
trails of blood coated with tan, powdery
medicine over ailing shoulder. Fifty years
        ago, this horn
was hers. Remarkably, with it, I hear
Starlight Airways announcing flight
        changes, which
causes an exasperated sigh from
transients standing on a moving sidewalk
that I, too, am on. Skimming through
a rickety tunnel decorated with flickering
        neon tubing,
a young, incense-peddling woman says,
"That's how cabin lights will be mid-flight
        over
the Caspian Sea." Fastened by safety pins,
a small stuffed monkey sits on her shoulder.
No one looks, except me. When she becomes
transfixed by the ear horn, I explain hearing
        aids funding
are due on my 64th birthday. Then, before
tucking her blissful-looking face into
        a military-style
shemagh, she looks coyly at her sidekick
and says, "Is your name Hey?"

2.

That's when I sensed—quite suddenly,
being under surveillance. Perhaps
     by airport
security or someone who might've
mistook me for the Cantaloupe Terrorist
seen that morning on bay area TV.
Cautiously, I step off the sidewalk
     to e-mail Zoryana,
who's apparently my contact. But she's
at the Western border with the Slavic
     NYC
Theatre. *"Since connections to Ukraine
are cancelled, the Ethno-Language
Conference is all but gone."* Sauntering
back to the concourse traffic, I soon
     notice
a burly shadow in the window's
reflection, disappearing behind others
     whenever
I pause to punctuate. *"Like a bannered
lance that's been left in a swamp
by a vanquished knight, does
bilingualism flourish thereto?
     Or does it
just collect itself to the brim
of an insect's oily eye
and sparkle conveniently?"*

3.

Later, after circling back to Gate 632
and losing a heavy-set man near
     customs,
I crab-scurry sideways to the nearest
bar for Singapore Slings. In an effort
to hide my bronze, tattooed face that's
highlighted with four pairs of silver
     earrings
outlining the rim of my ears—top

to bottom, *ancien regime* style,
        I stake
the drink's umbrella between gold teeth
and pop it open. Taking quick, methodical
sips with candy-striped straw, I physically
recoil at the conference agenda where
        culturally-
impaired types will pitch wares via
comedy, academia, governance,
        and books
on unbelievable beliefs deemed
"marketable and therefore
accessible." Nothing to despair
over—really, except the chicken
        kiev,
koulebjaka, and most notably
the vareniki.

4.

Another email, apparently the second
set of closing lines for the play, is drafted
        for Zoryana.
"Such pathos, my dear friend,
is indifferent because it'll seep through
the pig-colored butcher paper anyway.
And if the insect loses its grip on Earth's
        upkeep,
when will the Hummingbird Moths strafe
the tall grass with tracer fire?"
To which she replies: "Edgar, those women
with designer glasses
        and scarves
inch forward, crouching behind
cars and cradling lances. Under a sky
ablaze with the fiery after-trail
of arrows that morph to Northern
        Lights
arcing to the Southern Horizon,
we ask Sister, 'Will the Sun side
        with us now,

knowing we're faithfully determined
to keep away those who conspire
to stop Him from crossing the Sky
at mid-day?'"

5.

Exhausted and slouched into a booth
like a medieval sculpture, I chant-talk
      a glacier-
welcoming song, the one that makes
bullets ricochet off apparel in fiery orbs.
But if they somehow pass through
the bamboo armor, I tell myself,
      implanting
themselves to sub epidermal depths,
sizzling and emanating stone-grinding
      smells, the barbed
trajectories will be massaged to less
vulnerable areas of the body.

6.

Jumping over psychiatry like a spotted
eagle whose samurai sword dissolves
      non-ordinary
intrusions to balanced proportions
of electrolytes on a four-day fast,
I vow to stand firm over ground,
water, and air, waiting for invisible
      pockets
of vulnerability. Yet, as precaution,
I reach into the beaded shoulder bag,
      making sure
the passport and boarding pass are still
there. "So what's the answer," I ask
a stranger who's shaking my arms
vigorously, "to the question on who
      made you
spokesperson of the great Great

Lakes Nation?" He grips my extended,
marbled hand and says, "Sir, yes—
in friendship, we're closing. But
      the answer
to your question might be
the Chief. Right?" With earrings
      chiming
against the cool ear-horn,
I lean out of the booth: "Yes,
maximus radius or vice versa
are words saber-flashing in
      my sleep . . ."

OBVIOUS FOR STARS ONLY

en route to the hotel
of medical necessity we travel
highway 6 again passing by
the rock quarry which still
    possesses
a haunting audible deepness
but this road fails in pretending
to be lonely and unused
because anomalous signs
    for
wayward celestial travelers
have been left near farm
driveways and fields

they're hallowed markers
people won't recognize nor
would they question them unless
they knew from experience
    a wooden
cylindrical post balanced
atop a dark gray boulder
and pointing southeast by
northwest is in fact
    a compass

but it's there unnoticed
by passersby and being held
by nothing no cement
no superglue only mystery
    makes it
endure harsh elements
including the snow's ethereal
    weight

or it's embodied in another
sign like the old corncrib
at four-county corners
which resembles a long

            distant
runner frozen for one
century in a fall with arms
extended to greet the green
and red earth while one leg
            is bent
and the other is lifted
skyward aligning itself
with the lead star

of the seven star siblings
he's the son who awaits
to cast father's medicine
one of seven gifts
            empowered
to divide the space
between them and their
now-vindictive moon
stopping her briefly
            with
weather or landscape
but long enough to flee
across the sky thereby
providing a lifetime
            of reasons
for listeners why there's
day and night via mythology
the verbal shrine that
memorializes everything
            that
took place here or what's
taking place now

RETORNA ME . . . CARA MIA TI AMO

1.

On the tenth anniversary of M&M's death,
John Whirlwind, an honorary grandfather,
retold a 1950s Indian Relocation Act story,
a time the federal government lured him
      to Los Angeles.
Shaking a newspaper saturated with flour
and baking powder into a billowing cloud,
he said in a radio announcer voice, "I went
West to learn the printing trade." Upon
      job-training
prospects, he related several families
from the Settlement also left for large
Midwestern cities. After a nearby train
drowned out the anecdote's preface,
      he fanned
the cloud away, pointing back over
his hunched shoulders: "On that
damned train I went, and never came
back—for a while." At family doings,
      his
"relocation" yarns were treated like
an intoxicated, unwanted guest.
      Sometimes
he probably was. "His Dislocation
Program ended when he got there,"
whispered women kneading dough
to shape over an overturned, wooden
      bowl.
"And why didn't he pick a closer city?"
Concurring, the kitchen helpers rolled
their eyes as they ladle-stirred pots on
the stove. Several mothers hoisted infants
      to their arms,
asking: "Is the corn and chicken done?"
or "Is the tablecloth on the floor for the kids
yet?" They scurried about, grabbing
silverware and wondering when

to politely
exit the room. In spite of their unease,
John Whirlwind was an omnipresence.
"For good reason," grandmother said.
"As Secretary of your grandfather's
          Chief's
Council, he wrote monthly letters
to Washington, D.C., protesting
          Tribe's
Constitution and its court, police,
and Indian agents." And greater
still, we were told, he once helped
ambush an owl-hooting sorceress
          crossing
a river bridge. "Let me go," she
pled in the night, "and I'll give you
witchcraft." When they removed
her shroud, her nose reportedly
          deformed
in the ensuing years of her capture.
In addition to being an appointed
letter writer and witch-catcher,
Whirlwind was also known
          as a pow-wow
singer. His repertoire included
Blackfeet music learned from
a performer who stopped by
while traveling with a wild
          west-type
show. The first time I ever
heard of Browning, Montana
          I never
thought I'd go there one day
to sing with Two Medicine Lake,
that I'd hang four colored pieces
of cloth around my family's
          home
as protection from negative
elements.

2.

As I watched the reactions grandfather
caused, I secretly ripped off golden
pieces of hot fry bread. Through
the activity, I soon noticed there
       was less
pantomime in grandfather's "verboir"
rehash. As a poet, I was attentive to his
linguistic skills and mannerisms. I'd
scribble archaic words in a pocketbook
       only to later
forget their grammatical context.
When kitchen utensils began clanging
louder than railroad crossing signals,
grandfather gruffly intoned,
       "She died
ten years ago!" which made men
watching baseball on TV in the other
room shout, "Who died?" Once they
heard, "My Mare-nin, boys! This
       month
years ago!" the raucous chatter
resumed. At parents' request gramps
       Whirlwind
sat in the kitchen corner to avoid
scaring small kids with his beaver-
gnawed cane. That afternoon, though,
W. C. Fields had a teardrop and he
       was sniffing
discreetly. Whenever adults grumbled
"his lies only get bolder," or "the only
fool in Kisko Creek Valley is here,"
I took him out for a smoke.
       "Don't listen
to that crap," I'd console. "*Esta bien,*
nephew," he'd say in Mexican. "It's
OK." We weren't related, but he also
called me son, grandson, or *pendejo*
       under
Grain Belt beer mizz. To me, his
regression stemmed from a Life

414

magazine, which was hidden in
a green tin box. "When the Grandfather
World calls," he'd philosophize
"the only thing nearby will be
        a magazine."
In time, from one Secretary
to another, his Motion had
a second.

3.

When I was about ten years old—and even
before, he'd sometimes unlock a wooden
chest to take out a tin green box that had
a rolled-up copy of Life. But the chest
        itself
was hidden under waist-high longhouse
platforms where the ceremonial eating
and singing was done. After unraveling
Life from deer-hide bindings, he'd deftly
        find a page
marked by a gold ribbon and whisper
emphatically, "*Ma na ke-me nwa ne ma ka.
No ma ke-i yo-ne ne bo-na i na – e sa ki ne
ke ni tti,* This is the one I love. For a few
        moments I died
once when she held my hand." After
placing bricks on page corners, he'd
croon Return to Me in Italian: "*Retorna
me . . . cara mia ti amo . . . solo tu, solo tu,
        solo tu,
solo tu, mia cuore.*" Next to the black-
haired Weeping Willow teacher, a twin
        of Superman's
Lois Lane, the blonde woman in Life
was more enchanting. In the longhouse
shadows, M&M's photograph seemingly
pulled down daylight from the ceiling
        portal,
including the spaces between

the wall boards, making her eyes
and pouting lips alluring. The story
was, they did a tribal round dance
      at Eagle Rock,
a Los Angeles suburb. Holding
up his arthritic right hand, he'd say
in a gravelly Don Corleone voice,
"Her hands were soft . . . as the palms
      of a raccoon."
Half a century later, I learned
she was featured in the premiere
issue of Playboy. But I first espied
her wearing clothes in Life issued
      the same year.

4.

In 1962, on a hot August afternoon,
Mr. Winkle, a blotchy-skinned Sunday
paper man drove up the dusty driveway.
"She died, captain," he announced
      through
the station wagon window. Initially,
grandfather continued hoeing mounds
of dry soil around the potatoes until
a near-whimpering sound
      next conveyed:
"Our sweet M&M is gone."
When Winkle's eyes looked up
from under the straw hat, they
welled up with huge tears,
      magnifying
the reddish-orange edges of his
baggy eyelids. Only then did
gramps cease hoeing to accept
Ambrose wine wrapped in
      newspapers.
"Jezus, Wink, no one ever
believed me—just you, that I
      was M&M's

Fred Astaire." "Son-bitch, Freddy,"
Wink despaired while feigning to hit
the steering wheel hard repeatedly,
"can you believe this?" Before
          asking items
be put on his tab till powwow,
Gramps said he heard about her
on the radio. With a face seemingly
aglow with red spiders, Wink nodded
          and slowly
backed out onto the main road,
taking the loss harder than Captain
Whirlwind.

5.

Before attending the 5 PM birthday party,
we painted souvenir spear shafts with dark
red, nose-stinging paint. Once dried we'd
lay these down on two connected rows
          of bricks.
Occasionally, he'd pause to drum on
a cardboard box with arthritically-bent
fingers, singing or composing a tribal
word-song silently. Once dried,
          silver
wooden spear points were tied to shafts
and decorated with beads, bells,
and feathers. If craft sales were good
during the tribal field days powwow,
          the cupboards
were stocked for months and credit
stood at the local hardware store.
And Sunday papers were delivered
twice. On the tenth anniversary
          of M&M's
demise, my cousins were playing
vinyl records by the open window,
          yelling,
"Captain Whirlwind, *Ke ne ta i* –

be se ta ke ko? Do you want to listen
to something?" Beyond the Settlement's
borders, it was the Chinese Year
        of the Water
Rat, a time President Nixon's bomb
sights were set on Haiphong while
the radio played Al Green's "Let's
Stay Together." On the marquis still
        was
"The Godfather" and gas was fifty-five
cents a gallon. Before dropping out
of Iowa City, I traveled to the University
of North Dakota for a poetry reading.
        Although
I missed Simon Welch and James Ortiz,
fellow tribal poets, I sang with a braided
gentleman named Whirlwind Soldier,
and I understood a Lake Agassiz
        canoe-
speaker's words that some inlets
in late spring could cool a six pack
        of Olympia.
And years ahead, a North Battleford
canoe-speaker would linguistically
defuse concern over a brother missing
from American Host Drum duties.
        That night
through the dancers' Grand Entry
dust, Bear Raking a Tree White
walked across the parachute-
covered arena. In Holland he
        visited Germany;
in Saskatchewan he spent part
of Saturday in Alberta.

6.

At 21, on the steps of "The Cave,"
a concrete storage facility built into
a large, wooded hill, an August 1960
issue of Life was given as a birthday

present—
three months in advance: Marilyn
Monroe was on the cover beside
a French male movie co-star. "That
Year," said gramps, "I was a pit diver
        in Los Angeles."
Thus, the day he chose to cease going
under giant roller presses to remove
steaming-hot, defective cardboard,
he joined his Mexican co-worker's
        family
for supper and drinks. In a homesick
spell, he also took a bus to a pow-wow
in Eagle Rock. And it was there,
during an elevated state of jolliness
        when
a rare chance arose. As hide drums
reverberated inside the warehouse,
        an entourage
of celebrities who were attracted by
the sounds of bells and tribal singing
came in by mistake. When they found
out they weren't at a wrestling match,
        their mirthful
shouts of disbelief stopped the drums.
Once word circulated a star was on
the floor, the announcer immediately
asked, "Before you go, may I have
        the honor
of your lovely hand in dance?"

7.

Amazingly, Marilyn accepted.
Seeing how the announcer struggled
through the crowd, gramps said
he simply strolled toward Marilyn,
        taking
a cowboy hat from a chair along

419

the way. After recalling a myth
about a mischievous Turtle who
thought a sponsor was pointing
    at him
as being the dance contest winner,
he proclaimed with a smirk, "Yes,
in the most heinous turtle degree,
I cheated by cutting in on a dance."
    Yet,
when facing the prospect
of eternal regret, he asserted,
round dancing with a movie
star was a crimeless, leg-melting
    experience.
For months thereon—especially
in reliving the event, he could
    almost
catch the wondrous scent
of womanly soap and perfume
wafting beside his undeserving
mug like golden sweet corn
    tassels.

8.

In 1979, after John Whirlwind left
earth, a song called "Round Dance,
Marilyn" was composed for this
phantasmagoric anecdote. It goes:
    Round dance,
round dance ina kwe ni. Round dance,
round dance, ina kwe ni. Round dance,
round dance ina kwe ni – ne me tto e ma,
Round dance, my gramps must've said to—
    Marilyn . . .
Marilyn Monroe, I mean. So-o-oo
sexy circa 1960 Eagle Rock pow wow
in L.A.

NYE WI MAMITTI NAKAMONANI, FOUR PEYOTE SONGS, CA. 1930

No. 768.10

Hey yo ta
a no ka ne kwa
Ketti Manetowani

Lead vocal of song by one singer sung
four times over with a rapid drum beat

Hey yo ta
a no ka ne kwa
Ketti Manetowani

Second: replication of song by singers

Hey yo ta
a no ka ne kwa
Ketti Manetowani
Hey yo ta
Ketti Manetowani
Hey yo ta
a no ka ne kwa
Ketti Manetowani
Hey yo ta
a no ka na kwa
Ketti Manetowani

Chorus on first verse

Ayo a kwi tti
ki ki wi ta
me to se ne ni wa
Wi nwa
ni a no wa tti wa
A no ka ne kwa
Ketti Manetowani

Chorus on second verse

The person who partakes
is being requested
by the Great Spirit

Translation

The person who partakes
is being requested
by the Great Spirit

421

The person who partakes
is being requested
by the Great Spirit

The person who partakes
is being requested
by the Great Spirit
The person who partakes
is being requested
by the Great Spirit
The person who partakes
is being requested
by the Great Spirit

Here above
is where you'll stay
The people
they are the ones
who will agree
is being requested
by the Great Spirit

No. 768.12

Ki ne wa be na

Ki ne wa be na

Ki ne wa be na
Ki ne wa be na
Ki ne wa be na
Ki ne wa be na

Me me tti ne
wa se ya wi
Ketti Manetowa
ki ne wa be na

We will see Him

We will see Him

We will see Him
We will see Him
We will see Him
We will see Him

At the last
daylight
(The) Great Spirit
we will see Him
We will see Him
We will see Him
We will see Him

No. 768.13

Wi na
wi na a i ya
ki ya na ni

Wi na
wi na a i ya
ki ya na ni

Wi na
wi na a i ya
ki ya na ni
Wi na
wi na a i ya
ki ya na ni

Ke tti
Ma ne to wa
a kwi na ha i ya kwe
wi na
ni na a i ya

He
will know how (to make it work)
our lives
He
will know how (to make it work)
our lives
He
will know how (to make it work)
our lives

(The) Great Spirit
As far as we are able to know how (to make it work)
He
will know how (to make it work)
our lives

No. 768.19

We na i
na ta wi no ni

We na i
na ta wi no ni

We na i
na ta wi no ni
We na i
na ta wi no ni
We na i
na ta wi no ni
We na i
na ta wi no ni
We na i
na ta wi no ni

Ke bya tti- atti mo e ko na na
e ke te ma ke si ya kwi
na ta wi no ni
We na i
na ta wi no ni

Apparently
this is medicine
Apparently
this is medicine
Apparently
this medicine
Apparently
this medicine
Apparently
this medicine

It came to tell us
that we are poor
Apparently
this is medicine

CONTEMPORARY MESKWAKI SOCIAL DANCE SONGS

The One I Live With

Me ko te we ni *we we ne twi*	*Lead vocalization to song* *four times over in medium drum time*
Me ko te we ni *we we ne twi*	*Second vocal, echo*
Me ko te we ni *we we ne twi* *Mekoteweni* *we we ne twi* *Me ko te we ni* *we we ne twi* *Me ko te weni* *we we ne twi* *Ne te na-wi tti aka* *Ne te na-wi tti aka*	*Chorus, first verse*
	Second verse follows

Your traditional dance dress (made of fabric) is beautiful Your traditional dance dress (made of fabric) is beautiful Your traditional dance dress (made of fabric) is beautiful Your traditional dance dress (made of fabric) beautiful Your traditional dance dress (made of fabric) is beautiful I said to the one I live with I said to the one I live with	*Translation*

One at a Time

Na ne ko te nwi
Na to me ko-ma a ki

Na ne ko te nwi
Na to me ko-ma aki

Na ne ko te nwi-hey
na to me ko-ma aki
Na ne ko te nwi-hey
na to me ko-ma aki
Ayoi-hey
Ni mi tti
Ni mi to
Ni mi ta

One at a time
call these dancers
One at a time
call these dancers
One at a time
call these dancers
One at a time
call these dancers
here
The one who's dancing
The one who's dancing for
The one dancing

Micah Rider's Song

Hi ho Silver
ne te na (wo)
ne ka to ska tte e mo

Hi ho Silver
ne te na(wo)
ne ka to ska tte e mo

Mi tta tti ba o (wa)
Mi tta tti ba o (wa)
Hey (we)'re gonna go riding-riding
Ne te na (wo)
Ni ka na

Hi ho Silver
I said to
my horse
Hi ho Silver
I said to my horse
A fancy run he
A fancy run he does
He (we)'re gonna go riding, riding
said (to me)

428

Listen to the Good-voiced One, ca. 1930

Be se de
me nwi tti mo ta

Be se de
me nwi tti mo ta

Be se de
me nwi tti mo ta
Be se de
me nwi tti mo ta
Be se de
me nwi tti mo ta

Me nwe i ka wi
mi ko na
te wi i ka na
me nwi tti mo ta
Be se de
me nwi tti mo ta

Listen
to the good-voiced one
Listen
to the good-voiced one
Listen
to the good-voiced on
Listen
to the good-voiced on

Drum good
for the feather
(on this) drum
The good-voiced one
Listen
to the good voiced one

429

NOTES TO "FOUR HINTERLAND ABSTRACTIONS"

1.

In July 2006, I read news online that a replica of a Tomahawk cruise missile had fallen onto a Bronx, New York, highway. Apparently, the vehicle transporting the replica three-thousand-pound military training missile got rammed by another vehicle. This catapulted the crated missile marked *inert* off the platform. Beginning with authorities, the incident got the news media's attention.

Eventually, from the moment the fallen missile headline was read, it included this Native American "word collector." A second look had to be taken, however, until the remaining words, "but it was a dud," placated the pause. By then, though, it made no difference; I was already caught.

From the Meskwaki Settlement in central Iowa, between two midwestern rivers, I reacted like a flathead catfish, tte kwa me kwa, *that's been snagged by a treble hook. Lifted upward in a cloudburst of silt to the sun-blinding surface, the news shook me from a deep, apathetic slumber. After being landed and rolled onto the beach, I gasped in shock thereafter as sand stippled my convulsive torso and gills abrasively.*

Metaphorically that's how I took the fallen-missile news. From there, a decision was made to compose a poem. Short of going on a crusade espousing the dangers of transporting dangerous materials, I cupped my slightly arthritic hands over a spark from which a literary-based effulgence might be ignited. Before that happened, though, there was contemplation.

While a downed replica missile caused alarm among authorities, it was my opinion that, regardless of what various agencies said, a public-safety issue had been uncloaked. Another accident could happen again, I postulated, with perhaps a different outcome. Further, due to America's supply and demand, no one knows what's being delivered by land, air, or water. The principles of economics simply take priority. Yet despite safeguards designed to prevent mishandling of dangerous cargo, such precautions were *still* subject to human error. Unfortunately, in society's perpetual learning process, I concluded there's no teacher like grief to change society's ways.

Basically, that was the stance assumed seven years ago. The prevailing rationale was, if all a self-described hinterland poet could do was chronicle a fallen replica missile, then that was his sole purpose. The task was to poetically reshape and retell the news in a way that would make the subject greater than itself. With tribal culture as part of the foundation, the missile was then constructed as a nonordinary weapon. In this context, whether the Tomahawk was fully armed or "inert," it could be depicted as a life-taking entity that was also capable of thought, speech, feeling, and action.

I can recall that summer day when I jotted down the *New York Times* headline: "'Missile' Falls on I-95 in Bronx, but It's a Dud Used for Exercises." Not long afterward, I wrote a vague, half-whimsical description in a haiku poetry format. In reference to the missile being literally on the ground, which is how I first visualized this bizarre, thought-provoking situation, the phrase *upside down* was also inverted like a concrete poem. In another haiku/concrete version, the name Tomahawk was inverted, with the trucks portrayed post collision.

Reuniting with concrete poetry after forty years was nostalgic, but it wasn't the public safety message initially sought. Eventually, when the king-of-revision crown was donned and adjusted before the mirror, three other poems were drafted. In the end, the inverted set of words that creatively highlighted public safety capitulated to surreal, animistic, and otherworldly imagery in a four-part poem.

Thus, in its final form, the first poem portrays the missile as being animated. As the Tomahawk hisses and billows smoke menacingly on the freeway, there's public concern. At a juncture when authorities contemplate nudging the missile's fuselage with yucca sticks that symbolize a gauntlet, reverence is extended. Words are solemnly recited and a gift is offered. As priestlike voices rise in unison above the traffic's noise— a sign that reconciliation is perhaps tenuous—the temperamental entity hears how a vulture sacrificed its once beauty to shape earth. It also hears how the power of a meteorite supersedes everything resoundingly.

2.

The second poem portrays a transcendent *wa se si* ("wah seh see"), or firefly, that interacts with young family members on a winter night. The progression of events starts with the weeping willow and the protections it can provide through prayer and faith. According to tribal-based belief, trees are principles in nature's realm. They are therefore spirits that hold their designated place by watching people and this earth. As long as they are remembered in prayer and ceremony, my grandmother instructed, they are here to assure believers safe passage. Shortly after the firefly appears to the children, a request in a prayer is made for the tree spirit's help. The tree is made aware that since infancy the children, through their mother's teachings, have taken part in longhouse ceremonies. Therefore, "wi nwa-ne na to se si ka wa ki, it is for them I am asking."

At different times in my own travels for school, tribal performing arts, and literature, these protections were extended by my late maternal grandmother. It was reassuring to know from high above the Atlantic Ocean, for instance, that an unseen spirit was invoked to provide safe airliner travel. Similarly, from the night of the firefly's visit forward, the weeping willow is asked to guard the children from any and all unexplained entities that may appear to them at home or elsewhere.

3.

The third poem highlights the firefly's visit. True story, at least for two siblings who were witnesses. But as quickly as events of that unusual night unfolded, all details were soon forgotten. Interestingly, the third sibling, a teenager, said he saw nothing. It's my belief that since the younger siblings couldn't comprehend the firefly's appearance as a real-life event, their unfamiliarity may have prevented further interaction. Any recollection of its anomalous presence dissolved. With nothing else to compare the winter firefly to, their inexperience may have acted as a shield.

From past encounters my companion, Stella, and I had with paranormal sightings, we knew some manifestations could induce a dream-like state. If traditional charms aren't worn as defenses or if the psyche is unprepared and weak, one's thoughts and actions are all but incapacitated. Ostensibly this may include memory. In retrospect, maybe that's how the children dismissed these sensory discrepancies.

The story.

On a cold winter night in 2012, three siblings were warming the dogs' food and getting ready to go outside. One sibling, however, left alone to check a barking dog. Once he got back inside, he calmly said, "A firefly is bothering Simon and he's jumping up, trying to bite it." Remarkably, he added, the firefly knew how far to keep away from the dog. After we told him to wait for the others next time, we said fireflies don't exist in winter. After checking the yard from the picture window, we advised the siblings to proceed. It was a mistake. Before sitting back down, we watched them walk toward Colt, another dog whose house was about seventy-five yards away. Incredibly, after the kids got back inside, they said the wa se si began flashing from inside a tree. Why didn't you run back and tell us? we asked in dismay. Shrugging their shoulders, the two siblings said nothing. Apparently, as they got close to the weeping willow, the *wa se si* came out from the branches, dropping close to the ground in multicolored flashing lights. It then sped in front of the house where we had been standing by the window a few minutes earlier. We called the tribe's police to have the yard spotlighted, but nothing was seen fitting the description we gave. Not long after this incident, there was a tribal community loss. We concluded that aside from the firefly being a nonordinary presence, it could have been a shadow or a soul en route to the Grandfather World.

4.

The fourth poem is an homage to a veteran or *we ta se* ("weh tah seh"). Years ago, I was downtown when one such person came home. It was a hot, breezy afternoon when a Greyhound bus dropped off an Indian soldier. With a duffel bag balanced on his shoulder, the soldier walked over to the shaded side of the street and headed my way near the tavern and pool hall. Once we recognized each other as former classmates, we smiled and shook hands. When he put the bag down and leaned against a storefront, he said in Meskwaki, "*Wa ba ta no-ma ni*, look at this." Clumps of reddish soil clung to his boots. "I've been traveling for over a week—and this stuff is still on me." Reaching down, he broke the dry soil into small clouds. As they floated away in the wind, I recall thinking they probably came from halfway around the world.

Over the next few weeks, we would meet by chance over drinks and smokes and laugh about growing up. Realistically, we were barely old enough to buy alcohol, and life had hardly begun. That fall, I went to Southern California for college, and I would not see him again. Forty years later, I would learn he had been tapped on the shoulder when his tour of South Vietnam ended. On the day he came home, he smiled as we conversed in Meskwaki, a Great Lakes Algonquin dialect. Basically, that's what I seek to memorialize: that the young military veteran and I, an aspiring artist, were once tilting Budweisers in the moonlight. Sometimes when I look up at the elegant shadow-casting clouds that float over the Settlement's wooded hills, I wonder if they've recently drifted over a mountainous jungle called A Shau Valley.

NOTES TO "CONTEMPORARY MESKWAKI SOCIAL DANCE SONGS"

"The One I Live With" is dedicated to Wa se ke kwa, the One with whom I have had the honor to live for over thirty years. My wife, Stella, and I live on the Meskwaki Tribal Settlement in central Iowa where we are parents to six children whose ages range from five to sixteen. When Wa se ke kwa, who is a master of these arts, is adorned in Woodland-style finery with floral motifs, geometric designs in beads, or embroidery, I not only praise her artwork but imply her physical beauty. The song is sung in a traditional Meskwaki medium-fast drumming speed and is enunciated accordingly.

"One at a Time" was composed in part in the summer of 2003 when the Meskwaki hereditary Chief was asked to resolve a tribal dispute of governance. This was historic because the sacred role of the hereditary Chief who founded the Meskwaki Settlement in 1856 had not been recognized in over a century. Each Chief or O ki ma is therefore summoned, one at a time. When framed in a tribal celebration during which contemporary dancers exhibit their skills individually the tribute is rooted in ethereality reached through the grace and physicality of dance. The song is vocalized in strong half-pitch and performed as a Northern Plains Crow hop dance.

"Micah's Rider Song" was made when my son, Micah or Ke tta tti—Ma kwa, Kind Bear, was three years old. While horses are rare today in Meskwaki society, Micah's interest for them was affirmed through an early TV character I knew, a white horse called "Silver." The horse would lift its front feet before galloping off with the Lone Ranger. I mixed that western theme with the "riding, riding" lyrics and intonations I once heard on a modern cartoon called "The Backyardigans." So this is a children's pow-wow song sung in a Northern Plains Crow hop beat style. At four, Micah starts this song at the drum, with his siblings making the formidable echo.

"Listen to the Good-voiced One" is a Meskwaki song that was first recorded by Martha Champion Huot Randall in the summer of 1928. This social dance song is distinct in that there are several similar-sounding versions. Together, they share a vocal pattern, but the lyrics and messages are different. In "Listen to the Good-voiced One," there are eight vocal syllables, with the last vowel-notes being extended. With song spelled close to what it sounds like, this song requests one listen to the good-voiced one and to drum good for the feather: *Beh seh tah way/ meh nwee she moo tah./ meh nweh e ka way/mi ko na/ teh weh e ka naw.* In 1987, the Woodland Singers recorded "The Meskwaki People's Song" that asserts: "Meskwaki—this is their song. Here is their song." In contrast, another version asks: "Listen to the unmarried woman. She's singing (as) back-up (to the singers at the drum)." It's my belief these songs have been in use for over a century. On behalf of my family and our relatives, including our children, who perform them, we pray all songs from the Meskwaki Settlement remain for another one hundred years. Especially those with words.

MESKWAKI: ITS SPELLING AND TRANSLATION

It should be stated the Meskwaki spelling incorporated in these four books is improvised. Likewise with the translations. In a writer's mind-set, creative expression is the foundation and vehicle. As a result, the way I hear, write, read, and translate Meskwaki may not be the same as my neighbors on Red Earth Drive. The range of linguistic proficiency is wide: Some can understand it, but cannot speak it, while others, like me, speak it but cannot write it fluently. Just as there are a few who can speak and write effectively in Meskwaki, there are many who are monolingual.

Somewhere therein lies my work.

Unavoidably, not only are there grammatical errors in my transcriptions, but also a tendency to expand the written thought process—even though the message might be brief. To linguists and language-enthusiasts, if my trail over this terrain is made less discernible, I have yet to fully harness Meskwaki in text.

At this writing, at sixty-four years of age, it's interesting to ponder how I first learned to communicate in Meskwaki at home, yet my first written words were English at school. For reasons that remain unclear to this day, my family didn't emphasize tribal spelling as much as they did its verbalization. Would it have made a difference? Perhaps. To see the application of the English alphabet in Meskwaki would have delineated the different ways traditional speech is implemented.

Since that didn't occur, on or about 1980, I began teaching myself how to write Meskwaki. Since then, inasmuch as I toil over the composition of English, there have been ongoing struggles with the First Language's transcription. I would offer in conclusion that my efforts as the third-oldest elder in the Kisko Creek neighborhood stem from a young man who simply stumbled upon poetry two thousand years ago.

That's where this journey began. To all who endeavor to travel with me—
through words—you have my deepest appreciation.

Ray Young Bear

ACKNOWLEDGMENTS

Acknowledgment is made to the following publications in which many of these poems first appeared:

WINTER OF THE SALAMANDER

Pembroke Magazine, South Dakota Review, Phoenix, Seneca Review, American Poetry Review, Northwest Poetry Review, Cutbank, Partisan Review, Dacotah Territory, Poetry Northwest, Phantasm, The Great Circumpolar Bear Cult, Anthologies: Come to Power, The Crossing Press, Carriers of the Dream Wheel, Harper & Row

THE INVISIBLE MUSICIAN

Akwekon: "Debut of the Woodland Drum"
Akwesasne Notes: "The Significance of a Water Animal," "All Star's Thanksgiving," and "The Language of Weather"
American Poetry Review: "From the Spotted Night" and "The First Dimension of Skunk"
Amicus Journal: "My Grandmother's Words (and Mine) on the Last Spring Blizzard"
Another Chicago Magazine: "Three Translated Poems for October"
Bloomsbury Review: "Green Threatening Clouds"
Caliban: "The Dream of Purple Birds in Marshall, WA"
Chariton Review: "If the Word for Whale is Right"
Greenfield Review: "Eagle Crossing, July 1975"
Luna Tack: "Three Views of a Northern Pike"
Manhattan Poetry Review: "The Personification of a Name"
New York Quarterly: "Fred Bloodclot Red's Composition"
North Dakota Quarterly: "Emily Dickinson, Bismarck and the Roadrunner's Inquiry"
Northwest Review: "A Drive to Lone Ranger"
Sonora Review: "Always is He Criticized"
Sulfur: "Nothing Could Take Away the Bear-King's Image"
Taos Review: "The Suit of a Hand" and "The Black Antelope Tine"
The Clouds Threw This Light: "Nineteen Eighty Three"
Tri-Quarterly: "*Wa ta se Na ka mo ni,* Viet Nam Memorial"

ACKNOWLEDGMENTS

Tyuonyi: "Race of the Kingfishers"
University of Portland Review: "Cool Places of Transformation"
Virginia Quarterly Review: "A Woman's Name is in the Second Verse"
    and "The Handcuff Symbol"
Wicazo Sa Review: "Colleen's Faith"
Willow Springs: "Quail and His Role in Agriculture"
Wooster Review: "Journal Entry, November 12, 1960" and "Meskwaki
    Love Song #1, #2, #3"

THE ROCK ISLAND HIKING CLUB

The Kenyon Review: "The Reptile Decree from Paris"
Virginia Quarterly Review and the *Wicazo Sha Review*: "The Rock Island
    Hiking Club"
Akwe:kon: "The Aura of the Blue Flower That Is a Goddess" and "January
    Gifts from the Ground Squirrel Entity"
Ploughshares: "Summer Tripe Dreams and Concrete Leaves" and "Father
    Scarmark—World War One Hero—and Democracy"
Callaloo: "Our Bird Aegis"
Solo: "Eagle Feathers in Colour Photocopy"
Witness: "The Mask of Four Indistinguishable Thunderstorms"
The Gettysburg Review: "The Bread Factory" and "For Lazy-Boys,
    Devoted Pets, Health, and Tribal Homeland Reality, or How We
    Are Each a Lone Hovercraft"
Flyway: "Poems for Dreams and Underwater Portals"

MANIFESTATION WOLVERINE

Yellow Medicine Review & The Iowa Review: "Contemporary Meskwaki
    Social Dance Songs"
The Iowa Review: "Lone Woman Swimmer of Henry County, Virginia"
New Letters: "From the Landscape: A Superimposition"
Prairie Schooner: "Kamden Quadrangle"
The New Yorker: "Four Hinterland Abstractions"
Blue Heron Review: "A Life-shaping Spoon"
Four Winds Literary Magazine: "The Lonely Crickets Theatre," "Foot-
    prints Made of Snow," "Obvious for Stars Only," "Listen to the
    Good-voiced One." "Nye wi Ma mi tti Na ka mo na ni, Four Pey-
    ote Songs"

ABOUT THE AUTHOR

Ray Young Bear is a lifetime resident of the Meskwaki Settlement in central Iowa. His poems have appeared in numerous magazines and anthologies, including *Virginia Quarterly Review*, *New Letters*, *Prairie Schooner*, the *Iowa Review*, the *American Poetry Review*, and the *Best American Poetry*, and have been collected into three books: *Winter of the Salamander* (1980), *The Invisible Musician* (1990), and *The Rock Island Hiking Club* (2001). He also wrote *Black Eagle Child: The Facepaint Narratives* (1995), a novel combining prose and poetry that was heralded by the *New York Times* as "magnificent." Its sequel, *Remnants of the First Earth* (1998), won the Ruth Suckow Award as an outstanding work of fiction about Iowa.

The recipient of a grant from the National Endowment for the Arts, Ray Young Bear has taught creative writing and Native American literature at numerous schools across the United States, including the University of Iowa and the Institute of American Indian Arts. A singer as well as an author, Young Bear is a cofounder of the Woodland Singers & Dancers, which performs contemporary and traditional tribal dances throughout the country.

EBOOKS BY RAY YOUNG BEAR

FROM OPEN ROAD MEDIA

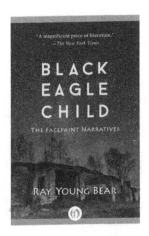 

Available wherever ebooks are sold

OPEN ROAD
INTEGRATED MEDIA

Open Road Integrated Media is a digital publisher and multimedia content company. Open Road creates connections between authors and their audiences by marketing its ebooks through a new proprietary online platform, which uses premium video content and social media.

Printed in the USA
CPSIA information can be obtained
at www.ICGtesting.com
LVHW091621300424
778917LV00005B/153